FIRESIDE

Books by Albert E. Kahn

Sabotage!*

The Plot Against the Peace*

The Great Conspiracy*

High Treason

The Game of Death

Days With Ulanova

Smetana and the Beetles

The Unholy Hymnal

*Joys and Sorrows—Reflections by Pablo Casals
as told to Albert E. Kahn*

With Michael Sayers*

Days with Ulanova

An Intimate Portrait of the Legendary Russian Ballerina

by

Albert E. Kahn

With an Introduction by
Arnold L. Haskell

A Fireside Book
Published by
Simon and Schuster

Copyrighted 1962 by Albert E. Kahn under the International Union
for the Protection of Literary and Artistic Works
(Berne Convention).
All rights reserved
including the right of reproduction
in whole or in part in any form
A Fireside Book
Published by Simon & Schuster
A Division of Gulf & Western Corporation
Simon & Schuster Building
Rockefeller Center
1230 Avenue of the Americas
New York, New York 10020
Layout and design by Albert E. Kahn and Edith Fowler
Manufactured in the United States of America

1   2   3   4   5   6   7   8   9   10

Library of Congress Cataloging in Publication Data

Kahn, Albert Eugene, 1912-
    Days with Ulanova.
    (A Fireside Book)

    1. Ulanova, Galina Sergeevna, 1910-   2. Dancers
—Biography. I. Title.
GV1785.U4K3   1978   792.8'092'4 [B]   78-14559
ISBN 0-671-24294-6 Pbk.

To Galina Ulanova

...the wonder of whose art, merged with her way of life, has brought a special beauty to our world—the present version of this book dedicated by the author on the fiftieth anniversary of her debut at the Mariinsky Theatre in Leningrad on October 21, 1928.

Contents

GALINA ULANOVA

An Introduction by Arnold L. Haskell

I *have been fortunate enough to have had some forty years of experience watching dancing all over the world and discussing the art with its greatest exponents. But I have the strong feeling that all my years of watching dancing have been a preparation for the few fleeting moments of watching Ulanova. Now, through this book, those moments are prolonged and intensified.*

My memories of Ulanova are, to me, a part of life itself, bringing a total enrichment of experience. To me, hers are not theatrical miracles but triumphs of the human spirit. Where Pavlova was supremely conscious of her audience and could play upon its emotions as upon an instrument, Ulanova is remote in a world of her own—which we are privileged to penetrate. She is so completely identified with the character she impersonates that nothing outside exists. The master craftsman by an act of humility has become the truth-revealing, life-giving art-

ist. When Ulanova takes her curtain call, it is immediately obvious that she has been called from afar, and that the salvos of applause are as much of an intrusion to her as they are to the more sensitive in her audience. For once this grateful noise seems horribly out of place.

Ulanova's complete concentration carries us with her through the period artificialities of Giselle *to a statement about life and love, through the highly skilled ballet-making of* Romeo and Juliet *to a true communion with the mind of Shakespeare. Working through the medium of what has sometimes been called the most sophisticated, stylized and artificial form of theatre, she has brought the dance for a brief moment back to its primitive origins in magic. I have felt, no, I feel, this strongly, for the enchantment persists. I have talked with Ulanova of her art; she is exceptionally intelligent and highly articulate. One has the strong im-*

pression that she would have succeeded in any walk of life—which explains the craftsman but leaves the artist a mystery. And what a superb craftsman, the most fluent and effortless exponent of the greatest of all schools of classical ballet, that of St. Petersburg—Leningrad.

There is, however, something revealing in her personality. The sense of dedication and integrity is common to all artists of the dance. With Ulanova there is the quality of exceptional humility, something quite distinct from modesty, and a feeling of completeness, a withdrawal into herself that can at times be strangely disconcerting through lack of contact. One can sense tremendous will, strength held in reserve. In no one have I ever been conscious of so great a feeling of power, of a powerful spring held in check. She safeguards her private life, her essential re-creation, with absolute determination, placing an implacable barrier between herself and all intrusion. Her very acceptance of grateful praise is coldly impersonal.

Her character reveals itself strongly when she is coaching a young ballerina. There is first the careful scientific explanation, and then, without any detailed demonstration of the whole, so as not to impose her own interpretation, she seems by a tremendous act of sympathy to inspire the pupil to dance. I must be careful not to suggest hypnotism, for the pupils are in no sense automata; it is an act of generous inspiration, a giving of self, and not a command.

Her beauty—and to me she is infinitely beautiful—is beauty of character and intelligence, a positive nobility that has nothing to do with accepted classical canons. It is as truly Russian as Pushkin or Tolstoy. Albert Kahn studied her for a long period and under all circumstances, following her so closely that she was no longer aware of his presence. The result is a complete record of an extraordinary personality. In this book there is the real Ulanova, as none but a few of her intimates can have seen her. I find it an inspiration not only for the memories that it underlines, but for the introduction to aspects of Ulanova I have never seen. I cannot conceive of a more precious or intimate document.

Theme and Variations

In the late spring of 1959 the Bolshoi Ballet came to San Francisco and concluded their first American tour, fittingly enough, in the city christened after the gentlest saint and set by the Pacific which in the name of peace joins their continent and ours. It was then this book had its conception.

I had met Galina Ulanova for the first time a few weeks before in New York. I happened to be there when the Bolshoi troupe arrived, and I sent her a note of greeting, mentioning I had visited Moscow the previous year as a guest of the Soviet Writers' Union. Knowing something of the demands of her schedule, I was surprised to receive a reply inviting me to call at her hotel the following evening. Hardly less surprising were my first impressions of Ulanova.

I am aware that the printed word and the truth are not necessarily synonymous, and so I had not been overly influenced by certain press reports depicting Ulanova as eccentric and aloof. Even so, I was hardly prepared for the striking simplicity and utter lack of pretension of this slight, clear-eyed woman in whom shyness and trenchant candor were strangely intermixed. Our conversation, which was made possible by the linguistic skills of a Soviet journalist, lasted for a couple of hours and covered a variety of topics, ranging from the respective merits of California and the Crimea to the question of whether or not Shakespeare's Desdemona was a courageous woman. (We agreed she was.)

Ulanova was to dance the next night in the Bolshoi's New York première, *Romeo and Juliet,* and she made no attempt to conceal her extreme nervousness. No fledgling ballerina before her debut could have been more apprehensive. She repeatedly returned to the subject of the opening. How, she asked, querying herself more than me, would an American audience react? Could Americans possibly have the same understanding as Russians of Soviet concepts of ballet? "Our approach," she said, "is different in so many ways from yours...."

Though feeling foolishly presumptuous, I tried to persuade her the performance would be a prodigious success. Having seen her as Juliet in Moscow, I said, I knew that the response to her dancing would be the same in New York. She banteringly replied that perhaps she would sleep better now.

Before leaving, I told her that when the Bolshoi Ballet reached the West Coast I'd like to take her and her husband sight-seeing in San Francisco. I came away aware that I had met a woman who was as extraordinary as she seemed ordinary.

By the time Ulanova arrived in San Francisco, her questions about American audiences had been emphatically answered. Perhaps never before in the annals of the American theatre had any troupe of artists received such ecstatic acclaim as the Bolshoi dancers. Everywhere there were overflowing halls and tumultuous ovations. Everywhere the critics exhausted their superlatives of praise and usually ended by saying no words could express what they had seen and felt. And everywhere the legend of Ulanova came alive for those who saw her dance. Their sentiments were perhaps best summed up by Harrison Salisbury of *The New York Times*, who described her as "the wonder of the world."

Between performances and rehearsals in San Francisco, Ulanova and her husband, Vadim Rindin, the chief designer of the Bolshoi Theatre, went sight-seeing with my wife, Riette, and me. And now I saw a new side of Ulanova. With the tour about to end, she was as gay as a schoolgirl on a holiday. A slender figure clad in trim sweater and slacks, the soft frame of her hair catching the wind, she gasped with delight as we drove up and down the city's cascading streets. She inquisitively probed the sidewalk displays of sea food along Fisherman's Wharf and wandered fascinated through the crowded byways and cluttered shops of Chinatown, affectionately teasing her husband for his inability to resist innumerable trinkets and souvenirs. Stopping to fondle a puppy, she spoke with some nostalgia of

her own dog, a poodle which had been sent her as a gift by a British newspaper. She had named it, she said, "Bolshoi."

When I marveled that she looked so well after the strain of the tour, she pointed to her muscles and declared, not without some pride, "I'm stronger than you think."

Rindin, genial and gentle-mannered, shook his head mournfully and said, "You can see why I'm afraid of her."

While conversation was possible only through an interpreter, who accompanied us on our wanderings, we were all familiar with the German for "beautiful"; and there were choruses of *schön* as, from various eminences around the Bay, we viewed the vast span of the sea and the massive, foam-rimmed headlands. If we lacked a common language, we found a swift rapport. We had been together only a short time when Ulanova said, "Let's not be formal. My name is Galya."

It was on our second day together that Ulanova and Rindin learned Riette was a sculptor and asked to see some of her work. Their response to it was warmly enthusiastic. Ulanova asked Riette whether she would like to sculpture her and added that she would be glad to pose if Riette could come to Moscow. Riette said she could think of nothing she'd rather do.

"Then it's decided," observed Rindin. And without more ado, as if Moscow were just around the corner, we began discussing plans for the trip.

When I suggested taking some photographs of Ulanova for Riette to use for purposes of preliminary study, she invited me to the Academy of the Ballet, where she was training while in San Francisco. There I learned that, notwithstanding her pre-eminence in the ballet world and more than thirty years of stage experience, Ulanova—whether she was at home or abroad—still attended a daily class under a teacher.

It was then, while watching her at the *barre*, that I first thought of doing a book about her—a book which, as I envisioned it, would be a photographic account of how she lived and worked. As soon as the practice session was over, I told Ulanova my idea. I had the feeling she was more amused than impressed by my ardor, but when I proposed working on the book in Moscow while Riette was sculpturing her, she replied, "Why not?"

There were various practical problems to be solved before Riette and I could head for Moscow.

Three of these problems were our three teen-age sons. What were they to do while we were away? After several family conferences, it was decided that the two younger ones would come along. The eldest would remain at home and continue his college studies.

Another problem was finding a sponsor for the trip. Taking along a one-page outline of my contemplated book, I went to Simon and Schuster Publishers in New York. The discussion with vice-president Peter Schwed and editor Charlotte Seitlin lasted barely half an hour. At the end of that time, Schwed asked me, "When do you want to leave for Moscow?"

That fall I visited the Soviet Union briefly to discuss some of the details of Riette's and my respective projects with representatives of the Bolshoi Theatre and the Ministry of Culture and to make arrangements for working and living facilities in Moscow. I returned to California to assist in the variegated chores of transporting our family overseas. Late in January, bearing a mass of baggage crammed with camera equipment, sculpture tools, schoolbooks and winter underwear, our safarilike quartet departed from our home, in Jack London's Valley of the Moon, on our eastward odyssey.

Stopping in Paris en route, we read the disconcerting news that Ulanova had just announced her retirement and would dance no more. A telephone call to Moscow established that, though Ulanova was temporarily indisposed with influenza, the report of her retirement was apocryphal. With a decided feeling of relief, we continued on our way.

In Moscow, we settled into commodious quarters at the National Hotel, overlooking Red Square and within a convenient two-block distance of the Bolshoi Theatre. Unforeseen events were to keep us there considerably longer than we had planned.

Riette and I had originally thought a period of three months would be sufficient for her to complete Ulanova's portrait and for me to get the photographs and research material for my book. But we had been in Moscow only a few weeks when misfortune struck.

The preparatory details of our work had been accomplished, our sons had started to attend a Russian school, and Riette and I were just settling down to concentrated work when, in swift succession, all four of us fell seriously ill. The sickness, a protracted one, ultimately resulted in our being hospitalized; and while the care given us was no less tender than efficacious, our confinement was scarcely conducive to creative work. Riette had to remain in the hospital for more than a month and was then too weak to make any significant progress on the Ulanova portrait during the balance of our stay in the Soviet Union. In fact, only now, as these words are written, is she completing it here in her studio at home. I was luckier and, after a spell of frustrating idleness, was able to get back to work. We stayed in Moscow until the Bolshoi season ended and then headed home.

Most of my photographs of Ulanova were taken during that five-month visit, although I was to make two more trips to the Soviet Union before finishing my work. In all, I took some five thousand pictures of Ulanova; and while the number seems sizable, I think I shall always be haunted by the irrecoverable moments I failed to capture. I saw so much of beauty in Ulanova, in her work, her way of life, and, especially, in her as a human being. The more photographs I took, the more I wanted to take; I became increasingly aware that I was entrusted with a task of more than immediate importance.

If I value my photographs of Ulanova, it is not because I happened to be the person who took them. It is because she is in them and because they comprise the only such record of her. While in the Soviet Union, I went through the photographs of Ulanova in various museums, the Bolshoi archives, and her own personal files; these collections contain only a few score pictures of her, mostly of the posed stage-portrait variety. There are some excellent motion pictures of her performances; but they cannot substitute for the photographic record of her career that might have been kept over the years, especially when she was performing more often than now. The absence of this record is not due to a lack of gifted Soviet photographers. Once I asked one of them why it had not been made. He said with a rueful smile, "You know how it is when you are very close to something beautiful, so close that you can reach out and touch it with your hand. You sometimes tend to take that beauty for granted, as if it will always be there...."

There is, I think, an additional reason for the paucity of photographs. That is Ulanova herself. For one thing, her single-minded devotion to her work has always made her impatient at any possible intrusion on it. For another, despite having spent so many hours on the stage before the eyes of hundreds of thousands of people, she remains essentially shy and withdrawn (qualities which perhaps account for her being sometimes considered aloof). She jealously guards her privacy and abhors anything that smacks of meretricious publicity. She has certainly never encouraged the taking of pictures, especially any of her personal life.

I have been asked why she then permitted me to take my photographs of her. Perhaps it was largely because the whole enterprise started in so casual a fashion and because in the beginning she foresaw its specific nature no more than I did myself. Certainly neither of us anticipated some of the problems involved in the undertaking.

I often had reason to recall a conversation with a Soviet publisher at an early stage of my work. "I wish you luck," he told me sympathetically. "Our firm wanted to publish a biography of Ulanova, and a very competent author agreed to write it. He came back after a few weeks and said, 'It's out of the question. She simply won't talk about herself — about her work, yes, but about herself, no.'"

There is nothing remotely coy or disingenuous about Ulanova's modesty: it is part of her very essence. If she recognizes in a strangely dispassionate way her importance as a dancer (and I am not entirely sure that she does recognize it), she attaches small importance to herself as an individual.

Indeed, I sometimes wished she were a little less modest. I could never get her re-

ally to understand why others might be genuinely interested in her as a person or why I wanted to photograph all possible aspects of her life. I once told her: "Galya, you take Juliet out of a book and bring her to life on the stage. I want to take you off the stage and bring you to life in a book. To create your Juliet, you have to know everything possible about her, including many things never seen on the stage; similarly, I have to photograph everything I can about you, even if much of it never appears in my book."

She said she understood, and I think she did—at least, for the moment. But within a matter of hours she had forgotten and was again asking how anyone could conceivably want to know what she did in her spare time or to see pictures of her exercising in the classroom. Time and again, even after she was so used to my camera as to be wholly oblivious of it, she would fail to notify me beforehand of some intensely interesting activity of hers, simply because to her it seemed commonplace and not worth mentioning; more often than not, I learned of such events entirely by chance. It was a problem I never fully solved.

There were also inevitable difficulties stemming from the fact that I spoke no Russian. I had the help of highly talented interpreters, to whom I am greatly indebted and without whom I would have been lost. Still, there can be no real substitute for direct communication.

On their last night on American soil in the summer of 1959, Ulanova and Rindin dined with Riette and me at a small café in Sausalito, a village which tumbles down the hills across the Bay from San Francisco. Slowly, the kaleidoscopic sky paled out stars sprang into the heavens, and across the water, like myriad fireflies, the lights of the city began to twinkle in the gathering dusk. "What a beautiful city!" said Rindin. He paused and then added, "What a beautiful land! What a beautiful world!"

And what beauty Galina Ulanova has added to our world!

If this book succeeds in communicating a portion of that beauty, it will have served its purpose.
                                                    A. E. K.

Chapter 1

"Talent Is Work"

Ah, but a man's reach should exceed his grasp,
Or what's a heaven for?

—ROBERT BROWNING

They tell this story of the famous Soviet writer Alexei Tolstoy. In the late 1920s, on the insistence of friends, he attended a performance of a young ballerina named Galina Ulanova who had recently made her debut at the Mariinsky Theatre in Leningrad. Afterward, his friends eagerly sought his opinion. He shrugged. "I don't know why you're so excited," he said. "After all, she's just an ordinary goddess."

The phrase has a felicity beyond its author's intention. For Tolstoy did not know Ulanova personally at the time and was speaking of her only as a dancer.

All humans are composed of contradictions, and most of all perhaps those rare artists of genius who conjure forth new richness from reality. Galina Ulanova epitomizes the paradoxical.

If her artistry seems sublime, she herself personifies humility; and if glamour surrounds the ballet, her way of life has an austere simplicity. To the classical expression of the oldest of the arts, she brings the tenets of a revolutionary new society. Shy as an individual, she bares her heart to multitudes. Gentle, she has an inflexible will. The celebrated effortlessness of her dancing is the product of prodigious effort; and, though physically delicate, she exemplifies the mastery of the body demanded by the spirituality of the dance.

The massive portraits of Marx and Lenin and the scarlet banners adorning the Bolshoi Theatre proclaimed the annual celebration of the Revolution of November 1917. Though it was the day before the holiday, widespread festivities were already under way. Throughout the city, factories, offices and schools were closed; all of Moscow seemed to be promenading in the frosty parks and snow-flecked thoroughfares. The members of the Bolshoi Ballet, too, were enjoying a respite from their daily labors. On this day there were no classes, rehearsals or performances at the Theatre. Except for pedestrians using its portico as a short cut from Sverdlov Square to Petrovka Street, the imposing edifice with its giant columns and rearing bronze horses was silent and deserted.

"Arriving at the Bolshoi this morning," reads the entry in my journal, "I couldn't find a soul. No attendants at the doors, no one in any of the administrative offices. Backstage, all was shadowy and quiet, not a stagehand in sight, no dancers hurrying to or from the dressing rooms. The building was strangely empty, lifeless and still. . . . Then I went upstairs, and there, in one of the classrooms on the fourth floor, I found Galya, all alone, exercising at the *barre*. She nodded at me without interrupting her work. After a while, she began practicing before the wall-length mirror at the end of the room. She worked for an hour. When we were leaving the building and walking toward the feeding spot of the pigeons that nest in the Bolshoi's eaves, I asked her why she hadn't taken the day off. She said with her little smile, 'I need the practice.' "

The episode was not exceptional. Repeatedly, when the Bolshoi dancers had a free day, I would find Ulanova practicing by herself in one of the dance studios at the Theatre. In fact, I came to regard this as quite natural. It was, if anything, the idea of her *not* working, even on holidays, that seemed unnatural.

To Ulanova, work is the decisive factor in all creative endeavor. "When does an artist's life begin?" she says. "It seems to be impossible to give a precise answer. And I don't see any need. Why try to explain the inexplicable? Let's leave that to the experts. But one thing is certain: whenever we dig down into the achievements of a creative artist, we invariably trace them to the beginning of all beginnings—labor."

Ulanova is not given much to writing; but in articles by her that have appeared over the years, one theme is always stressed —the paramount importance of work. And characteristically, while famed for the lyricism of her dancing, she talks about a dancer's work in terms far more realistic than romantic. "Whenever I think of my apprentice years they appear to me as one long period of plodding, work of the arms, legs and body—an everlasting grind at the *barre*. Just as a man cannot live without bread, talent cannot exist without constant work. The realization that your labor has brought delight to people is the best reward for all the tortures of endless rehearsals, for all the innumerable and often fruitless experiments, searchings, tests in preparation of each new role. . . ."

A favorite quotation of hers is Maxim Gorky's phrase: "Talent is work."

"All dancers are hard workers—they have to be," I was told by the ballet director, Vladimir Preobrajinski, formerly a leading Bolshoi dancer and partner of Ulanova. "But with Ulanova, work is—well, you might say sacred. Nothing—no joy or sorrow—can keep her from her work."

I had not been long in Moscow before I realized Ulanova was reluctant to have me attend her daily practice sessions. Each time I suggested coming to her class, she put me off with some excuse. She would invite me, instead, to a rehearsal with one of her partners, or she would belittle the interest of the work that day in the class.

Finally I learned the reason from my interpreter. "If Albert comes to the class," Ulanova had confided to her, "he'll concentrate on photographing me. There are excellent dancers in the class, and I'd find it embarrassing if he took pictures of me and not of them."

Only after I told Ulanova I intended photographing not just her but the class as a whole did she set a day on which, providing the *maître de ballet*, Asaf Messerer, had no objections, I could start photographing her practice sessions.

Six days a week, usually from ten to eleven in the morning, she attended a class under the supervision of the lithe, quiet-spoken Messerer, a former Bolshoi dancer of great fame. (On the seventh day, she could often be found practicing alone in the classroom; she took perhaps two days off a month.)

No distinction was made between Ulanova and the other members of Messerer's class, which included not only outstanding soloists but dancers from the *corps de ballet*. Together with them she went through *barre* exercises and center practice, and, like them, she received periodic instruction and criticism from Messerer.

"When I have something to say," Messerer told me, "she listens with the utmost attention. She's very self-critical and very receptive to criticism. Considering her greatness as a dancer, she might be vain. But she's just the opposite. You might say she exemplifies humility. It's typical of her that when she starts work she goes through all the exercises like any pupil. However, she does nothing formalistically. She tries each day to improve every movement—and, in fact, she affects the character of the whole class by her presence."

"But how can anyone teach *her* anything?" asked my sixteen-year-old son Timothy, who became something of a balletomane during his months in Moscow.

While the question is understandable, it is certainly one which never occurs to Ulanova. "I shall never stop learning," she says. "I think I shall always feel like a student."

For me, Ulanova's daily practice sessions were a never-diminishing source of wonder (a fact which caused her no small amount of wonder). While her classroom work was unquestionably the "grueling labor" of her own down-to-earth characterization, it was also an enthrallingly creative process. The aesthetic was inseparably interwoven with the ascetic; she imparted to the strictest exercise a special loveliness. In all the weeks of watching her practice I cannot recall a single careless gesture. Even the positions she assumed in moments of repose had a haunting grace, as if, instinctively, her body sought and shaped the beautiful.

She worked with a consuming and infrangible concentration that one felt from the moment she entered the studio and started exercising in her dark leotard and loose-fitting warm-up stockings. Whatever exercise she performed, no matter how elementary or complicated, that instant had an urgency, as if everything depended on it and she were inwardly taxing herself to the utmost. Other members of the class would greet visitors cordially, or casually converse with them during work intervals. But I never saw Ulanova interrupt her work to speak with friends or acquaintances who occasionally came to the classroom. She might acknowledge their presence with a nod, but that was all; usually she did not talk to them until the class was over. Between exercises, she would sometimes stand at the edge of the floor chatting with her colleágues; but I always felt that unless she was discussing some aspect of the work at hand such amenities involved a conscious effort on her part.

At the *barre* and during center practice, her expression had a quality—an intensity and austerity—that I observed in the face of no other dancer. Or, I should say, no other *adult* dancer. Oddly enough, I saw a similar expression in the faces of children exercising at the Bolshoi School of Ballet. Perhaps the affinity was more meaningful than strange. Perhaps it signified that throughout the years, Ulanova has never lost that pristine passion and dedicated zeal, that devouring absorption and wonder of discovery which enable the child to find a whole world in a sunlit mote and forever in a moment.

When I developed my early photographs of Ulanova working in the classroom, I could not understand why she was so disconcertingly small in them. Obviously they were taken from too great a distance. But why was this so? There were ample opportunities to get close to her.

Then I realized what the trouble was. I was afraid of her, afraid of this slight, fragile woman who had seemed so girlish to me when I had first come to know her. Or, to put it more precisely, I was fearful of doing anything that might in any way interfere with her work. With considerable effort and self-admonition, I forced myself to get closer to her during her practice sessions. After a while, in fact, I had moved sufficiently close so that one morning she almost collided with me while performing a series of *fouettés*. "You startled me," she told me later that day. "When I'm spinning, I always try to keep my eye on some object to avoid getting dizzy, and

suddenly there you were and I thought I was going to hit you."

I said I'd been frightened too, but by the possibility of interrupting her. "The fact is, Galya," I confessed, "that I'm often afraid of you in the classroom. I'm afraid of intruding on your work."

Her expression indicated both surprise and a certain delight at the idea. She said facetiously, "If you want to increase your knowledge of ballet, perhaps you should intrude more."

But I was no more capable of following that advice than she was serious in giving it. As a matter of fact, even after I came to be accepted as practically a classroom fixture, I never felt completely at ease while photographing Ulanova during her practice sessions. I relaxed only at the end of the class, when we usually enacted a little ritual: knowing her partiality for sweets, I would then present her with one of the English mints I kept stored for her in my camera case.

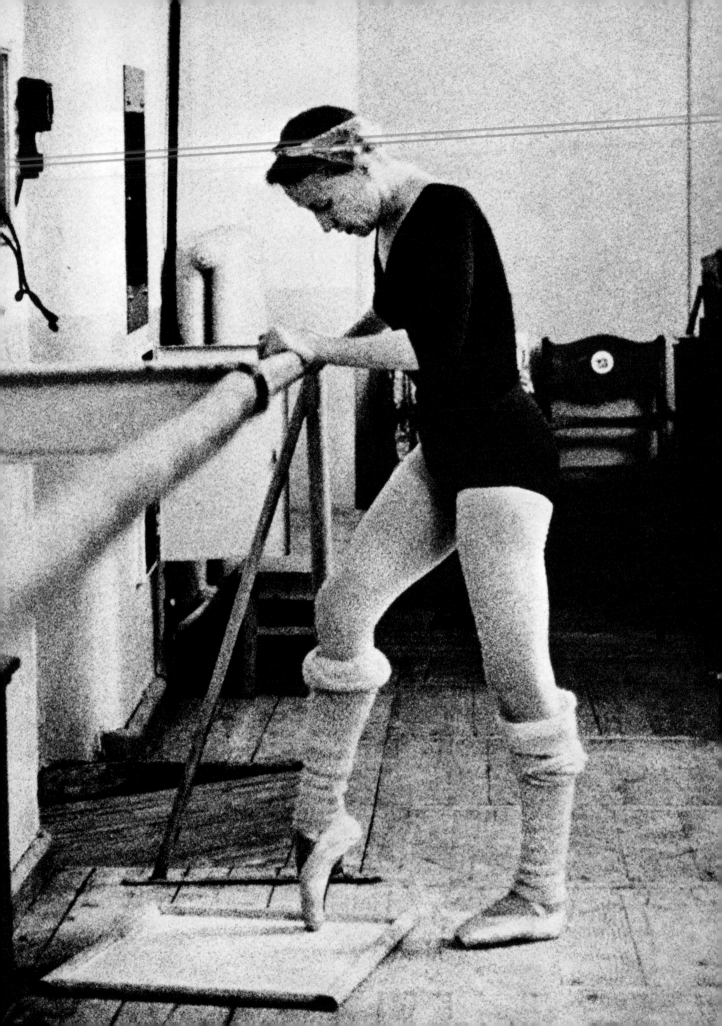

There were two occasions on which I saw Ulanova's concentration slightly disturbed during her classwork.

I was responsible for the first. One morning, to photograph the class from a particular angle, I had climbed on top of an old cupboard behind the practice mirror, which reached almost from the floor to the ceiling. All at once, with a horrendous crackling, the cupboard's top gave way, and like a vanishing genie I plunged from view. At my abrupt disappearance, there was a burst of laughter from the class; when I hoisted myself back up to my previous vantage point, I was greeted with applause. Ulanova was still performing the exercise she had been doing a few moments before. She did, however, pause long enough to shake a finger at me in mock reproof.

Another morning, during one of the magnificent national dance festivals that are periodically held at the Bolshoi Theatre, a group of children from Moldavia was rehearsing in the studio adjoining the one in which Messerer was conducting his class. Somehow the children learned Ulanova was in the next room. Immediately, despite the efforts of several adults to stem the tide, they swarmed into the room, and there they remained for the balance of the session, clustered around the piano and behind the *barre*, watching Ulanova with enraptured expressions. While other members of the class were clearly distracted by the lovely little visitors and paused to chat with them, Ulanova's attention remained on her work, as she continued exercising before the mirror. But I noticed that occasionally a slight smile flitted across her face. And when the children surrounded Ulanova at the end of the class, she chatted animatedly with them before going to her dressing room.

20

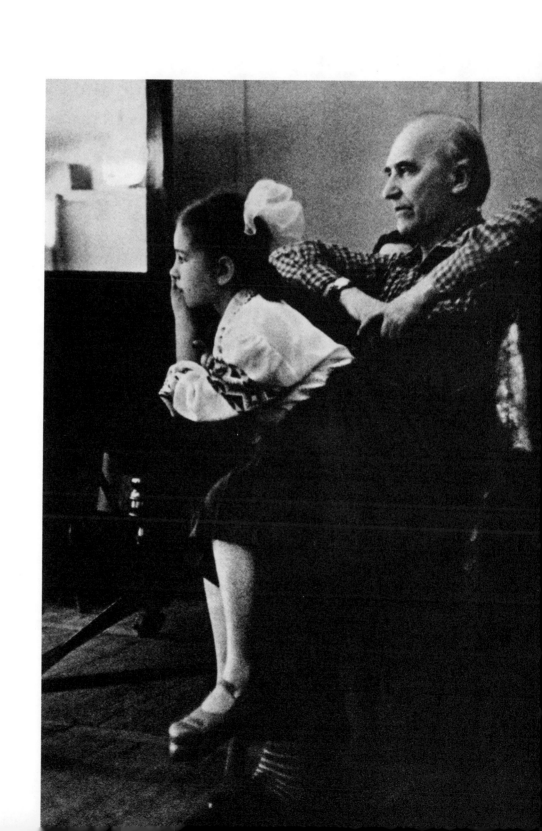

130501

Chapter 2
The Magic Word

What is your substance, whereof are you made,
That millions of strange shadows on you tend?
—WILLIAM SHAKESPEARE

To make music visible is the dancer's task," says Ulanova. "The dance is the embodiment of music in movement." In this metamorphosis, the dance acquires a language of its own and speaks, for all its silence, with a soaring and no less universal eloquence.

Ulanova thinks very consciously of the dance as a language, a means of specific if special communication. While noting that the analogy must not be carried too far, she observes, "Just as letters go into the making of words, and words into the making of sentences, so separate movements combine into the 'words' and 'sentences' of the dance, which form the poetry of the choreographic tale." She sees the language of the dance, like the spoken word, as related to human progress. "It may be vastly varied and can and should develop in the same way as living human speech, which is enriched and changed by the course of time, by the development of society, by the regeneration of a people's social and spiritual life." At the same time, it has the function of voicing profound unchanging truths. "For me, the value of my work lies in the conviction that the language of the ballet can convey to people great and vital truths about life, about the beauty in life and in the human heart."

Like the greatest poetry, Ulanova's dancing speaks a language understood not only by trained aesthetes but by ordinary working men. The universality of her message lies in its direct communication with the human heart. Her dancing is both a testament and a song: a testament to a way of life and a song to life itself. It is not only beauty in movement that she brings to the ballet; it is the beauty in man.

To Ulanova, technique represents "the ABC of the dance," which a ballerina must "know by heart and be able to handle as freely as a good pianist handles the keys of a piano."

She adds: "What is essential, it seems to me, is to command technique with sufficient freedom to enable you to express the principal idea of the dance—the boundlessness of the feeling in Juliet's heart, the tremulous transports of Odette's love. Moreover, technical perfection should be such that the public should never notice, never suspect that any of the movements cost the dancer the least strain. The dance must flow smoothly in clear-cut, finely traced lines, like those which stamp the work of great graphic artists."

I was often reminded of that image while watching her rehearse for performances. It was as if I were viewing, in swift succession, a series of old-master drawings, exquisite sketches forming the matrix of the final canvas. But Ulanova herself never appeared satisfied. It was not merely that she sought an ultimate mastery of every technical detail. That surely was part of it, but one sensed much more. There was a pervasive quality of quest and exploration, and, at the same time, a certain element of puzzlement and frustration, as if she were constantly searching for some ever-evasive answer, pursuing some ever-elusive goal.

Her repertoire while I was in Moscow consisted of three ballets: *Chopiniana* (known in the West as *Les Sylphides*), *Giselle* and *Romeo and Juliet*. She had danced in these ballets scores of times over the years. Yet at each rehearsal one might have thought she was preparing for a first performance. She would repeat the same movements and scenes over and over again, and, almost invariably, at the end of the session engage in an intensive review of the rehearsal with her partners and her coach, the former Bolshoi dancer Tamara Nikitina.

"When she comes to rehearsals," I was told by the Bolshoi dancer and choreographer, Alexander Lapauri, who had frequently partnered Ulanova, "it's as if she leaves the world behind. Some dancers are moody, eccentric, temperamental. Nearly all have their emotional ups and downs. I've been working in the theatre fourteen years, and I've often seen ballerinas cry, because they were dissatisfied with their work, or because of tension, or because the strain just became too great. I've never seen anything like that with Ulanova. If she has personal problems, you never know it when she's working. She never shows it."

There is, however, a deceptive quality to this seeming equanimity; and a significant side light on Lapauri's observation is shed by Ulanova herself. "Even now, at times," she relates, "I find it very hard to work at rehearsals. People are watching, they speak of commonplace things, and I feel I cannot do anything. I feel ashamed. It's different during a performance. There I don't see the audience. My partners, while they're still the same individuals, become something else and assume the features of heroes...." If Ulanova seems imperturbable at rehearsals and gives the impression of leaving the world behind, it is due not to anything of the automaton in her but rather to her extraordinary self-discipline and restraint, which are surely no less painfully exacting because of their imperceptibility.

Ulanova's associates repeatedly told me how unsparing of herself she was when preparing for performances. I heard one story from Leonid Lavrovsky, the chief choreographer of the Bolshoi Theatre. "It was when we were in Yalta making the film of the ballet *Romeo and Juliet*," he related. "You know the moment—Ulanova has made it famous, of course—when Juliet runs across the stage on her way to Friar Laurence. Well, the Bolshoi stage is about twenty-five yards wide, and the distance she had to run in the film —we were making it out of doors—was considerably more. It was seventy or eighty yards. The first time she ran it when we were rehearsing before shooting the scene, I said there was something that didn't seem quite right to me. So she ran it again—and again. In fact, she ran that distance nine or ten times—almost half a mile—before we realized what the trouble was. She was running into a wind and over ground that sloped slightly uphill, and her skirt was lifting a little too much, making her knees visible. And that's what was giving a slight awkwardness to the run. We reversed the direction, and then it was all right.

"A group of sailors was watching the rehearsal. Every time Ulanova made the run, they applauded loudly. But after a while, they began to get worried, and one of them said to me—quite seriously, too—'If you kill her, we'll kill you!' But Ulanova would have run the distance ten more times to make the scene exactly right."

The pictures on the immediately following pages are of Ulanova rehearsing with Rima Karalskaya and Nicolai Fadeyechev for the ballet *Chopiniana*.

Watching Ulanova prepare for a ballet, one is likely to become so absorbed as to forget its multiple components, to which her own artistry is inseparably joined and without which, indeed, it could have no fulfillment. She herself, however, never forgets. Her colleagues extol her remarkable individuality as a creative artist, but she constantly emphasizes that the beauty of the ballet is the achievement of the labors of many. "Credit for that beauty," she once wrote in an article addressed to young aspirants of the ballet, "must go to the hard work of hundreds, no, thousands of people, from the dance instructors who train the artists to the performers, producers, composers, scene designers, property men, electricians, stagehands, costumers, make-up artists, shoemakers, seamstresses, engravers, carpenters, and so on, ad infinitum."

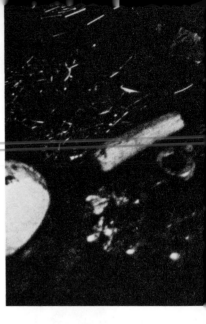

There can be no more vivid proof of that point than a visit to the Bolshoi Craft Shops, an extraordinary if little-publicized institution located on Moskvin Street, adjoining a pillared edifice in which Napoleon is said to have stayed overnight a little more than a century ago during his brief, ill-fated visit to Moscow.

The modest phrase "Craft Shops" is decidedly misleading. This unique establishment is a five-story factory employing five hundred full-time workers and carpenters, wigmakers and costume partments in which ninety-one different trades are practiced. They include the crafts of metalworkers and carpenters, wigmakers and costume designers, dressmakers and turners, tailors and chemical workers, painters and joiners, electricians and embroiderers, construction workers and mechanical engineers, scenery designers and sculptors. Typical workers are the sprightly eighty-one-year-old tailor Piotri Ivanovich Fomichev, who strikingly resembles an older Khrushchev; Yevdokya Shetova, whose production of ballet shoes includes fifteen pairs a month for Ulanova (the ballet-shoe department as a whole turns out seventy-two pairs a day); and Olga Ivanova, who has worked in the plant for over thirty years and makes *tutus* for all Bolshoi prima ballerinas. One huge room, reaching to the roof and having a floor area the size of a football field, is topped by catwalks from which artists and stage designers get a panoramic view of backdrops spread out on the floor five stories below.

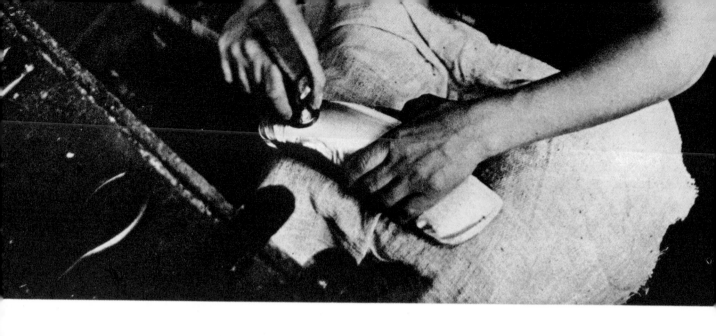

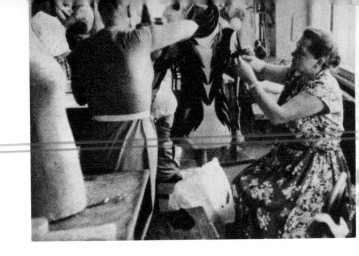

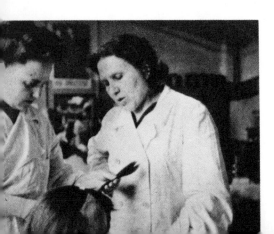

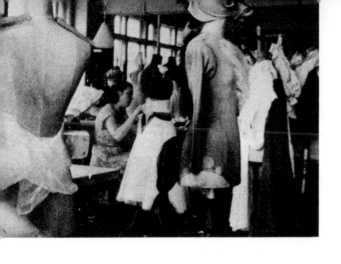

"I am very fond of Chopin," says Ulanova. "I first became acquainted with his music in the thirties. It's more than thirty years since I heard Vladimir Horowitz's concert, but it still seems a very short time ago. He spent a whole evening playing works of his favorite composer. And it was really unforgettable. . . .

"In 1926, when I was a student at the Leningrad School of Choreography, I danced Chopin for the first time. The scherzo was produced on the little stage at our school. Naturally, my knowledge of music was limited, but the production pleased me enormously; its melody, its lightness, carried me away. Two years later, a few months before graduation, our group began to rehearse *Chopiniana*. I danced one of the mazurkas in the 'Seventh Waltz' at the graduation performance. I was beside myself with fear and couldn't understand how I came through the performance. The 'Seventh Waltz' was to remain in my repertory for life, and I still always dance it with great absorption.

"In spite of the absence of a plot, the music of *Chopiniana* is so good, and the dance expresses it so fully, that when the spectator sees the performance he forgets there is no plot. He seems to be seeing a living embodiment of alluring, romantic daydreams. And that's the great charm of the ballet."

Every performance of Ulanova at the Bolshoi Theatre is regarded as an occasion of special significance. Nor is this mainly because her appearances are now infrequent, sometimes only once or twice a month; rather it is because of the realization that each of her performances is a precious work of art, unique in itself. The moment that it is announced she is going to dance, all tickets disappear as if by magic.

One of the highest compliments that can be paid a visiting dignitary in Moscow is to be taken to one of Ulanova's performances. "I have known foreigners," relates Harrison Salisbury, former Moscow correspondent of *The New York Times*, "who reckoned the length of their stay by the number of times they had seen Ulanova. 'How long have I been in Moscow?' one of these would say. 'Well, I have seen Ulanova in *Swan Lake* twenty-four times. I have seen her in *Romeo and Juliet* fifteen times. Just about six years in Moscow, that's all.' "

My pictures of Ulanova in *Chopiniana* were taken just thirty-two years after her first performance in this ballet at the time of her graduation from the Leningrad School of Choreography.

42

"If I were asked what new element the Soviet era has contributed to the ballet," says Ulanova, "I would put the spectator first." In contrast to Czarist days, when the ballet was the special province of the nobility and the elite, the Bolshoi audience now largely consists of the most ordinary Russian citizens, whose interest in the ballet rivals that of Americans in baseball. At Sunday matinees, children—who are not allowed to attend evening performances—occupy most of the seats and, during the intermissions, virtually take over the Theatre's buffets, where the two most popular commodities are ice cream and caviar.

Members of the audience promenading during the intermission cluster interestedly around a display of the Bolshoi's first American tour, which is among various exhibits in a room off the main foyer.

"*Giselle*," says Ulanova, "is one of the ballets which has won my heart. Changes in repertoire often separate us from our favorite productions, sometimes for long periods. That happened with *Giselle*. For several years I didn't dance in it. But when I returned to it after the production was renewed, it was like meeting with an old friend after a long separation and discovering new and finer qualities."

She continues: "In *Giselle*, I was faced with the problem of portraying love—hopeful and radiant in the first act, tragic in the second, but in both acts so powerful that it is able to conquer death itself. This is the significance of *Giselle*; the ballet is not merely a repetition of a simple maid's seduction by a wealthy noble—those who think so err on the vulgar side.

"My Giselle was conceived as follows: A young, carefree girl, in love and convinced of her happiness, experiences a great tragedy and in the end develops into the tragic image of a woman with a great suffering heart. In rehearsing *Giselle*, I tried to conjure up that image. I sought instinctively for that something, that 'magic word,' if you like, that would turn me into Giselle and make me live her tragedy and believe in it so utterly as to make the audience believe in it too."

In the following pages, Ulanova is rehearsing *Giselle* with Fadeyechev.

54

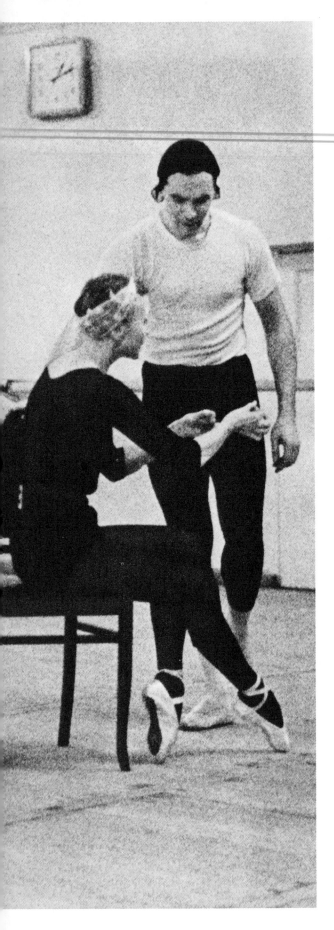
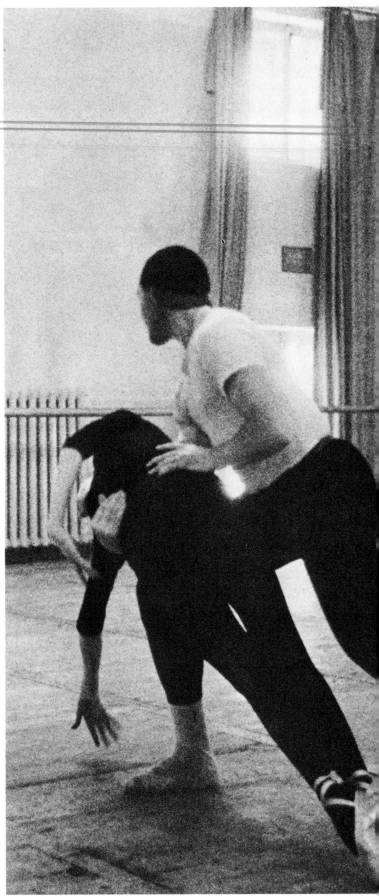

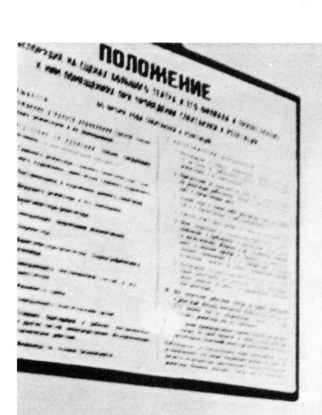

It was shortly after arriving in Moscow that I first saw Ulanova dance in *Giselle*. Immediately before the performance, Lavrovsky helpfully suggested certain scenes and episodes on which he thought I should concentrate in photographing Ulanova. I wrote them all down and carefully reviewed my notes when I got to my post at the prompter's booth in front of the stage footlights. The house lights dimmed, Yuri Fayer led the orchestra in the brief dramatic overture, the curtain rose on the bucolic, sunlit village. . . .

The moment Ulanova appeared on the stage and began dancing I forgot everything Lavrovsky had told me. I was seized by the feeling that every instant had to be caught and recorded, or else it would be irrevocably lost and gone forever. This was due not only to the wonder of Ulanova's dancing; I was, in fact, less conscious of that than I had been during rehearsals. Now I was living through an amazing experience which transcended the dance. The romantic fable was forgotten; the idyllic setting and fairy-tale costumes faded away; I was sharing in the essence of an ageless truth, an infinitely compassionate comment on the happiness and sorrow of life itself.

All at once, in the middle of the first act, something went wrong. Ulanova's image suddenly became indistinct in my camera; and frantically as I tried to adjust the focus, she remained blurred. Then I realized that the fault was not the camera's. My vision was obscured by tears. I made a determined effort to thrust my emotions into the background and concentrate on taking pictures. It was no use. To photograph Ulanova I had to watch her, and watching her made photographing her almost impossible. I did the best I could under the circumstances.

Between acts, I again saw Lavrovsky. "I've seen her dance *Giselle* many times," he said, shaking his head in wonder, "but this is one of her most inspired performances." As I left him, he said, "Tonight you must photograph everything."

But his advice once more proved ineffectual. I saw most of the second act in a blur.

Chapter 3

Science of Life

Dancing...is no mere translation or abstraction from life; it is life itself.
—HAVELOCK ELLIS

For Ulanova, the beauty of the dance is an expression of the beauty of life, and the creation of the one requires the assimilation of the other. "The artist must love life and have the ability to observe it," she says, "to see it in its infinite variety, to focus attention not on the banalities, not on the seamy side of life, but on all that is bright and beautiful, all that is useful and necessary to one's work."

Nothing is more alien to her than the concept, voiced by a recent writer on the dance, that ballerinas "are a highly specialized breed, selected and developed for a rarified, artificial purpose... and little else in life matters to them." Ulanova writes, "The work of the dancer is not only physical. The intellect has its share in whatever the ballet dancer does. The dancer will think independently and boldly, will have broadness of vision, only through assimilating life's experiences and mastering the greatest of all sciences—the science of life."

There was a time when her innate shyness and the exacting discipline of her work stood between her and the outer world. "In general," she relates of her youth, "very active and full-blooded people had an overpowering and depressing effect on me, and at first I avoided them. But later I began to understand they were helping me, teaching me to react differently to the world."

Today, Ulanova finds no hiatus between her art and the world about her; the two, for her, are inseparably interwoven.

The windows of Ulanova's apartment on the ninth floor of a towering apartment house overlook the Moscow River, the clustered buildings of the sprawling city, and, southward, the gleaming turrets and slender spires of the Kremlin.

Each morning she leaves the apartment house around half past nine. Her destination is always the same—the Bolshoi Theatre.

(A revealing incident occurred in connection with the preceding photograph of Ulanova looking out of her apartment window. Being invited to meet with Premier Nikita Khrushchev as my work in Moscow drew to a close, I was going to give him this photograph as a present. I asked Ulanova to autograph it. At first she readily agreed, but then she demurred. "He's a very important person, you know," she said seriously. "And it seems to me—well, I think it would be an immodest thing for me to do...." When I presented the unautographed picture to Premier Khrushchev and told him what Ulanova had said, he nodded, smiling. "Yes," he remarked, "she's a very modest woman.")

The Bolshoi Theatre of Opera and Ballet is aptly named. In Russian, *bolshoi* means "big." The Theatre, with its multiple ramifications, is a city within a city. Its total population, including artists and technicians, teachers and administrative officials, students at the Bolshoi School and workers at the Bolshoi Craft Shops, is almost three thousand. Its domain encompasses, besides the great Theatre itself, rest homes and vacation resorts near Moscow and on the coast of the Black Sea, kindergartens and summer camps for children of its personnel, its own library, newspaper, museum and polyclinic.

In the workings of the Theatre, Ulanova's part is not only that of a prima ballerina. As Chairman of the Bolshoi Ballet Council, one of the Theatre's three main governing bodies, she plays a leading role in the programming of performances, the casting of dancers, and the general supervision of the company's affairs. "In no sense is she a figurehead," I was told by Georgi Orvid, Director of the Bolshoi Theatre, himself a Council member. "She has the same serious approach to organizational matters that she has to dancing, and there's no phase of the company's work about which she doesn't concern herself."

In the discussion with Orvid and Vladimir Preobrajinski on the following pages, Ulanova was stressing a favorite theme of hers: the importance of developing young dancers and giving them, as soon as they show competence, leading roles. Neither of her colleagues was in disagreement with her, but she expressed herself no less emphatically on that account.

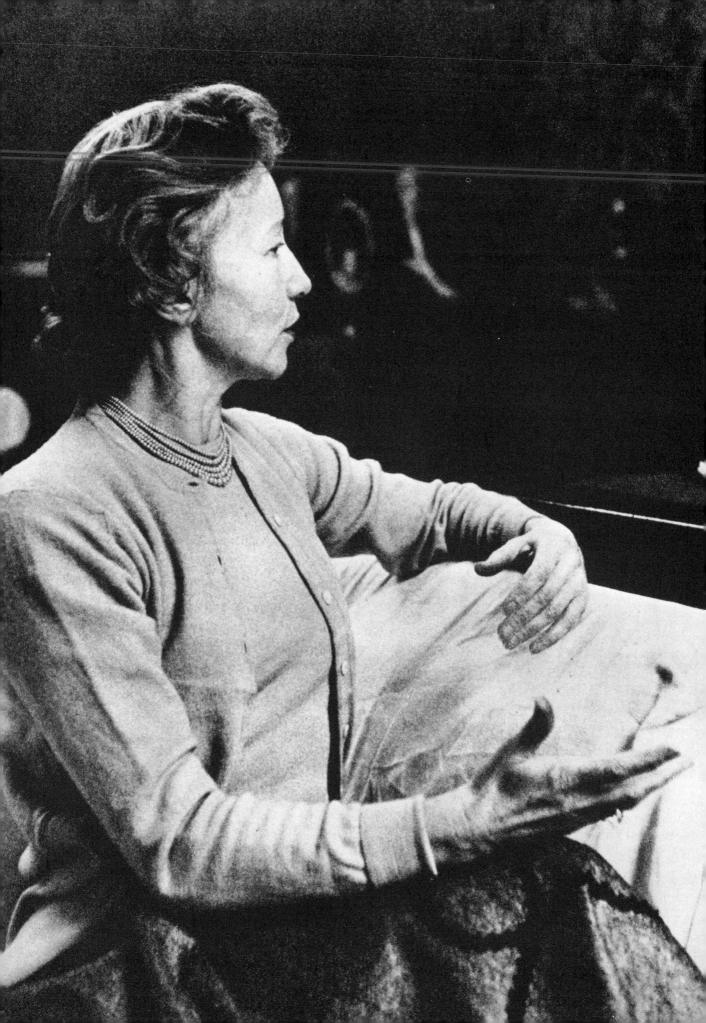

Almost invariably when there was an important rehearsal Ulanova could be found watching it; she rarely failed to have some discerning suggestion for improving the production. On this day, the company was rehearsing Lavrovsky's new ballet, *Paganini*. Together with her husband, Vadim Rindin, who had designed the sets for the ballet, Ulanova studied every phase of the rehearsal; from time to time she joined Rindin and Lavrovsky in animated discussion. After the rehearsal, Ulanova and Marina Kondratieva remained in the auditorium working out some changes in the young ballerina's costume.

The past reached hauntingly into the present when Romola Nijinsky, widow of the great Russian dancer Vaslav Nijinsky, visited Ulanova one afternoon at the Bolshoi Theatre. They had met fifteen years before under unforgettable circumstances.

"I believe," Madame Nijinsky relates, "it was the most astounding experience in my husband's life since he ceased to dance."

Nijinsky had left Russia in 1911 at the age of twenty-one, never to return. He had subsequently married the young Hungarian dancer Romola de Pulszky. They had been married only five years when Nijinsky's meteoric career was brought to its tragic end by insanity; and thereafter his wife devoted herself to his care, never relinquishing

the hope—bolstered by his periods of lucidity—that his illness might be cured.

The end of the Second World War found the Nijinskys in Vienna. One night they were invited to attend a theatrical performance under the auspices of the Red Army Command. The events of that evening are described by Romola Nijinsky in her book *The Last Years of Nijinsky:*

"Upon our arrival at the Ronacher Theatre we were led to a box near the stage. The house was crowded by members of the Red Army. . . . The program of the performance was not announced. Before the curtain was raised a young Russian officer came in. He bowed before Vaslav and said in Russian, 'This performance is given as a surprise for you. We hope you will approve and

enjoy it.' . . . We had never believed that from the ruins of Vienna would arise such an amazing expression of the art of the dance. As one ballet followed the other, we could hardly believe our eyes, and unheard-of enchantment unfolded before us. Vaslav and I looked at each other. Then he drew his chair nearer the stage and forgot everything around him, gazing at Galina Sergeyevna Ulanova, enthralled by her dancing. . . . All of the great women dancers of the past were embodied in her form.

"Vaslav . . . gazed and gazed at the stage and applauded through the intermissions, just as a young, enthusiastic student would have done. The performance was concluded by Fokine's *Sylphides*, which Vaslav had created with Kar-

savina. As they started to dance the variations, Vaslav clutched his hands and followed each step, accompanying their dance with a perceptible movement of his body."

The following day Nijinsky and his wife visited Ulanova at her hotel. "Officers of high rank, soldiers, mingled with the artists waiting in the hall. They greeted us with tears in their eyes, their arms full of red roses. . . . We followed Galina Sergeyevna into her apartment. . . ."

A few years after that memorable encounter Nijinsky died in London, and his widow settled in the United States. Now, a decade later, she had come to the Soviet Union to discuss making a film about Nijinsky's life.

The conversation between Romola Nijinsky and Ulanova took place in a small room opposite the Bolshoi director's office. It was a gray, overcast afternoon. A wan light reached through the window and softly illumined their faces as they talked.

After telling Ulanova about the plans for the Nijinsky film, Madame Nijinsky said that she was presenting the Bolshoi Theatre with four notebooks of Nijinsky's memoranda on choreography and that she was giving the theatre in Leningrad the costume in which he had danced *Le Spectre de la Rose*. "I'm going to send here the sculpture Rodin did of him," she added.

"Wonderful!" Ulanova said. "What size is the sculpture?"

Madame Nijinsky said it wasn't large and indicated its height.

"We treasure everything we have of your husband," said Ulanova. "He's like a legend for us."

As the conversation drew to a close, Madame Nijinsky murmured, as if to herself, "*C'est comme un rêve.* Yes, like a dream. I can't believe that I am here."

When Ulanova left the Theatre after a day of work, young girls were often waiting at the stage door. They would shyly murmur their greetings, thrusting flowers at her as if eager to be rid of them; as she took the small bouquets, smiling her thanks, she seemed somehow to share their embarrassment. I once started to photograph this little ceremony, but Ulanova, seeing me raise my camera, said quickly, "Please, no." So I limited myself to photographing the girls looking through the car window as we drove away.

No matter how brief her absence from the apartment, Ulanova was always welcomed home by her dog Bolshoi as if she had been to the other end of the earth. Barking and twisting from head to toe, he would prance ecstatically about her, then scamper off to fetch tennis balls and other treasured tokens of affection. She reciprocated by cradling him in her arms and whispering confidences in their own private language. When she went through her mail, Bolshoi would enthrone himself in her lap, his button eyes gleaming with delight. "He's my rival," I was told by Vadim Rindin. "It's a triangle. . . ."

The mail brought letters from all parts of the world—invitations to perform in different countries, messages from ubiquitous admirers, proposals of articles and press interviews, and requests for pictures, autographs and advice. The correspondence on this day included a communication from the American Academy of Arts and Sciences notifying Ulanova that, along with Pablo Picasso, Pablo Casals and several other notables, she had been elected an Honorary Foreign Member of the Academy; a request from a teen-age girl in Kew Gardens, New York, for a signed photograph; a cable of greetings from a balletomane operating a health farm in Australia; and a letter from Hans Hansson, head of the Sea Rescue Service of Göteborg, Sweden, urging Ulanova to dance in his country and, if possible, to give a benefit performance for his organization. "If you could make such a gesture," wrote Hansson, "for the benefit of this service for the safety of sailors, fishermen and travelers over the Baltic Sea, it would make a lot of goodwill. . . . If you could possibly come to Sweden, I promise, dear Madame, that your charming person will be received with great pleasure, love and adoration."

Though Vadim Rindin's working day was divided mainly between the Bolshoi Theatre and its Craft Shops, he spent considerable time drawing and painting in his study-studio at the apartment. A prolific and versatile artist whose career in the theatre started with painting stage scenery in the days of the revolution and civil war, Rindin had designed sets for some two hundred different productions in the intervening years. Notwithstanding his extensive duties as chief designer for the Bolshoi, new creations of his were constantly appearing in other theatres as well. The productions staged with his sets and costumes while I was in Moscow included the ballet *Paganini*, the opera *War and Peace*, and the plays *Vanity Fair*, *Hamlet* and *A Winter's Tale*. Remarkably enough, despite all this productivity, he never gave the impression of being under pressure or, indeed, even very busy. Soft-spoken and gentle-humored, he had a witticism for every occasion.

When I took the photograph on the left, Rindin was finishing a stage design to send as a gift to the Palace of the Legion of Honor in San Francisco. Before inscribing the painting in English, he took off his glasses. "These are German spectacles," he said and, putting on another pair, added, "I think I should wear my English ones for this."

When I learned one day that Ulanova was to confer with the Minister of Culture, Ekaterina Furtseva, I asked the Minister's permission to photograph the meeting. She, however, demurred. While showing a warm interest in the Ulanova book, she evinced a reluctance to being photographed and a modesty not unlike Ulanova's. "After all," she said, "your book is about Ulanova, and I don't know why anyone will be interested in seeing my picture in it." Only after I pointed out that the meeting was illustrative of the close working relationship between the Bolshoi Theatre and the Ministry of Culture did she consent to my presence.

The meeting took place in Madame Furtseva's office at the Ministry. The discussion, which lasted an hour, was largely about ballet teachers and the problems arising from the fact that a number of outstanding teachers, like Asaf Messerer, were now abroad, helping establish ballet schools in other countries.

At one point, the conversation turned to methods of teaching. "Our trips abroad and our contacts with Western countries," said Ulanova, "have shown us that they've learned from the Russian ballet school; but at the same time we've seen that there are things we can learn from them."

When Ulanova mentioned the need for improving the facilities of the Bolshoi School, Minister Furtseva remarked, "It won't be difficult to build a new school. With the present construction program and building techniques, we can soon take care of that." (Not long afterward, plans were under way for the construction of a new school almost twice as large as the existing one.)

Toward the end of the discussion, the subject of my book came up. "It's a pity Albert didn't have more of a background in ballet," said Ulanova. "It would have helped him."

"I liked the pictures he showed me very much," said Minister Furtseva. "He has a serious approach."

"Well, he's stubborn," said Ulanova.

Ulanova's appearances at receptions and similar social functions are rare. One such occasion was a reception for the American financier and patron of the arts Robert W. Dowling, who had figured prominently in the promotion of American-Soviet cultural exchanges. The reception was attended by Soviet cultural celebrities and guests from the American Embassy, including Ambassador Llewellyn Thompson.

An ebullient man of varied interests, Dowling took Ulanova aside as soon as she arrived and began expounding one of his latest ideas. He wanted, he told her, to arrange the production of a film based on pictures from my book about her. With Tamara Mamedova (a former Soviet cultural attaché in the United States) acting as his interpreter, he launched into a vigorous description of the film as he envisaged it. His enthusiasm made him oblivious to the decidedly unfavorable impression his proposal was making on Ulanova. When he paused at last, she turned to me and said, "Your book isn't even finished yet, and you're already talking about a film! One thing at a time is enough. And anyway, I'm against the idea. A film like that would be completely static."

I assured her that my sole concern at the moment was finishing my book and that the film idea was entirely Dowling's; and as Dowling, undaunted, continued explaining the merits of his project and Ulanova continued belittling them, I withdrew a few steps to photograph the debate.

The group was joined by Madame Nina Popova, hostess of the reception, and the well-known Soviet film director Sergei Gerasimov, who delighted Dowling by supporting his contention that effective motion pictures could be made with still photographs. Ulanova, however, remained unpersuaded.

Finally, Dowling said, "Madame Ulanova, will you answer me one question?"

"Of course."

"I'll concede that if you're really opposed to the film you have the right to deprive thousands of persons of seeing your own person. But let me ask this—do you have the right to deprive them of the chance to see your dog, Bolshoi?"

Ulanova joined in the laughter. "I give in," she said. "Go ahead and make the film."

With such frequency did Sol Hurok appear in the USSR—arranging American tours for the Bolshoi and Leningrad Ballets, for the Moiseyev dancers, for Oistrakh, Gilels, Richter and other Soviet artists—that he gave the impression of commuting between Moscow and New York.

No matter what the immediate purpose of his visit, he always sought out Ulanova. "I've worked with a lot of great artists, from Chaliapin and Pavlova until today," the remarkably youthful, seventy-three-year-old impresario told me. "But Ulanova— Well, she's unique. Don't ask me what it is, because it's a lot of things. But I can tell you this. She's one of the most undemanding persons I ever knew, and when there's a job to be done there's nothing she won't do to help.... When I brought the Bolshoi to America last year, I read a newspaper story saying she only dances when she feels like it. You know how many of the company's performances she danced in on that tour? More than half of them—more than thirty out of sixty! Sure, it was her first time in the United States. But it wasn't just that. She knew how important the tour was. I don't mean just to her as a dancer. I mean because of the need for our countries getting to know each other. Believe me, she's worth more than all the diplomats put together."

My interpreter was not with me when I photographed a meeting one evening at the Bolshoi Theatre between Ulanova, Hurok and Orvid. Their conversation was in Russian; and afterwards I asked Hurok what Ulanova and he had discussed.

"I was asking her," he said, "when she would come back to the United States. She said, 'When you invite me.' So I invited her."

"I was brought up on Tchaikovsky's music," Ulanova relates. "It is part of my very being. It has always been associated with my work, from the first time I danced Odette-Odile in *Swan Lake* at the Mariinsky Theatre, and Princess Aurora in *Sleeping Beauty*, and Masha in the *Nutcracker*. It's not only Tchaikovsky's ballet music that I love. I listen to his symphonies with never-diminishing delight."

Ulanova was listening to the finale of Tchaikovsky's Fourth Symphony when I took the photographs on these pages. The occasion was a concert at the Bolshoi Theatre commemorating the fiftieth anniversary of Leo Tolstoy's death.

"I was seated beside Galya in the director's box," I noted in my journal later that evening. "She swayed slightly to the music, moving her fingers in small rhythms, a little smile betokening the treasure of some inner secret, her features and hair softly limned by the light from the stage. So as not to disturb her, I held my camera in my lap and trusted to luck, fervently hoping to catch something of her mood and gentle movement."

Occasionally, when not at the Bolshoi or some other theatre, Ulanova and Rindin spent an evening at home with friends; and sometimes my wife Riette, the boys and I shared the evening with them.

Sitting around a table bright with flower-bedecked china and laden with a copious variety of cakes, cookies, fruit and candy (both Ulanova and Rindin having a special weakness for the latter), we would enjoy a late, leisurely, characteristically Russian repast, which was gaily reflected in a large wall mirror. Ulanova was a busy and solicitous hostess, hurrying to and from the kitchen, constantly replenishing supplies, making sure that the boys, especially, were fully satisfied, and, at the same time, not neglecting the dog, Bolshoi.

Bolshoi's appetites were various. He not only consumed with dainty relish the cookies, neat slices of apple, and other tidbits with which Ulanova plied him—he also had a taste for human apparel. My first time at the apartment, he had—from a strategic position under the table—deftly and unostentatiously devoured a portion of Tamara Mamedova's skirt while she was absorbedly interpreting a discussion on contemporary art. Thus alerted, Tamara had suggested to our boys before their first visit that they keep a careful eye on Bolshoi and divert his attention whenever he seemed about to satisfy his hunger for clothing. Actually, the instructions proved unnecessary, as the instant rapport between Brian and Bolshoi kept them both busily engaged throughout the evening.

Chapter 4

City of Birth

O! she doth teach the torches to burn bright.
—WILLIAM SHAKESPEARE

There is a magic and majesty to Leningrad, a haunting loveliness. Every palace and river bend, every monument and cobblestone evokes the memory of the past and the promise of the future. For here, with the storming of the Winter Palace on a chill autumn night in the fateful year of 1917, the past was ended and, from the city's womb, the future of the nation was born.

"I remember well enough," Ulanova writes of the city of her childhood, "the police search of our rooms in the summer of 1917 and afterward the flaming banners of the Revolution."

The earth-shaking events of those days left a special imprint on the seven-year-old girl, whose parents were ballet artists at the Mariinsky Theatre. "Besides dancing at the Theatre, they gave free recitals at night before film audiences, like other artists seeking to bring art nearer the people. I remember my father carrying me, frozen and sleepy, from a recital, through the bitter-cold, snow-swept city. With no one to care for me at home, my parents had to take me with them. I can still see Mother changing to her ballet shoes from clumsy felt boots and tying the pink ribbons with stiff, numb fingers in a cold cubbyhole behind the film screen. She came on stage with a smile. But I saw how tired she was and what a strain it was for her to dance....Back home, she made our simple supper and put me to bed. I woke often and saw Mother working—washing or hanging clothes to dry, or mending or sewing. I felt she never rested and never slept."

Ulanova recalls that when told she was to be taught to dance, she cried out in anguished protest, "I don't want to!" But simply because her parents had nowhere else to leave her, she began boarding and studying at the Mariinsky ballet school.

Thus, during the harsh winter of the Revolution and the grim ensuing epoch of intervention and civil war, there were sown in the beleaguered city the seeds of a legend of surpassing beauty.

When Leningrad was besieged by the Germans in 1941, the members of the Kirov Theatre (formerly the Mariinsky) were evacuated to the city of Molotov in the Urals. Ulanova relates, "The evacuation was part of our government's program to protect the arts, even in the midst of war. Actually, I went first to Moscow. There was a meeting of Allied leaders there, and I remember Winston Churchill came to one of our performances. The performances started at four in the afternoon because of possible bombing at night...."

Throughout the war, Ulanova danced frequently before Red Army audiences. "From our fighting men at the front," she relates in an autobiographical sketch, "we received daily corroboration of how dear the theatre was to them.... The men who wrote to me were strangers but they were as dear as brothers...." She cites one letter as an example. Written to her by a soldier in a village just cleared of Nazi troops, it read: "In one of the cottages we found a picture of you as Odette in *Swan Lake*. The picture has a few bullet holes but all the same the boys took it to their quarters, and while we're having a lull the orderly's standing assignment is to place fresh flowers in front of it every day."

The war years inevitably affected her work as an artist. "I felt drawn more closely than ever to the people. They were giving their all, spiritually and physically, to the war effort. The realization of this led me to dance Juliet differently after the war. I now put greater emphasis on such features in Juliet as moral courage and resolve."

The Leningrad chapter of Ulanova's career ended during the war. Early in 1944, she permanently joined the Bolshoi Theatre.

Today, though Ulanova speaks with marked nostalgia of Leningrad, she seldom visits the city. And this, perhaps, is due not solely to the exigencies of her work but also to the somber memories that are interwoven with the bright. "My happiest summers," she once told me, "were spent at Lake Seliga, not far from Leningrad. The little village there was completely destroyed during the war. It has been rebuilt, but I've never been able to bring myself to go back...."

Once during my stay, late in April, she paid one of her infrequent visits to the city of her youth. It was more or less by chance that I learned she was going. The day before, she casually mentioned she wouldn't be practicing the following

morning as she was leaving Moscow for a day or so. When I asked where she was going, she said to Leningrad. She was, she added, taking part in a concert in honor of one of her former colleagues, Robert Gerbek, who was retiring after thirty years on the stage. I promptly reserved a seat on the night plane to Leningrad.

My journal contains these notes: "At the airport, I find Galya is on the same flight. Before take-off, an airport official tries to place Galya in front of the line of waiting passengers, but, typically, she objects to 'special treatment.'

"In the plane, she rummages intently in her purse, finally finds the object of her search, and offers me—a stick of Spearmint chewing gum. It's one of the few times we've been together without an interpreter, and we converse in monosyllables and sign language during the flight. I have with me *Wilson's Dictionary of Ballet* and show Galya her biographical entry and photograph. She examines the little book curiously, lingering over the pictures of Pavlova, Nijinsky and other ballet greats, and then, coming on some drawings of basic ballet positions, she shakes her head, borrows my pencil and proceeds to correct them.... She seems unusually relaxed, perhaps because she's getting away briefly from all her responsibilities in Moscow. Her mood reminds me a bit of the way she was in San Francisco. She recalls America for a different reason. As we approach Leningrad's myriad scattered grains of light, she exclaims, '*Schön!* Los Angeles! New York!'"

Awaiting me at the Leningrad Airport were my warmhearted hosts of a previous visit to the city, Helen Konstantinova, Chairman of the Language Department at the Conservatoire, and Helen Petrova, Assistant Professor of English and American Literature at a teachers' college. As we drove off after leaving Ulanova, who was met by friends, the two Helens chattered excitedly.

"It's a gala occasion!" said Helen Konstantinova. "All Leningrad is talking about it."

I asked why this particular performance was so unique. They looked at me in amazement. Didn't I know that Ulanova was to dance the wedding scene from *Romeo and Juliet*, and that her partner would be Konstantin Sergeyev of the Leningrad Ballet, who had been Ulanova's first Romeo twenty years before? No, I admitted somewhat sheepishly, I hadn't known. Mentally, I thanked my lucky stars that I was there.

The morning after our arrival in Leningrad, Ulanova rehearsed with Sergeyev. The rehearsal took place at the ballet school (in one of the classrooms) where, more than thirty years before, Ulanova had learned to dance.

Word that she was coming had spread through the school, electrifying children and adults alike. Whispering pupils clustered expectantly in the corridors; teachers went about their work with ill-concealed excitement.

While Ulanova was doing her warming-up exercises, a door leading onto the balcony overlooking the classroom inched open and a group of girls silently materialized in the doorway. Spellbound and motionless, like a fragment of some classic frieze, they watched Ulanova. When Konstantin Sergeyev joined her and the two went to another room to rehearse, the girls tiptoed after them, to congregate in the doorway there.

The rehearsal was brief. It lasted perhaps less than half an hour. But in that particle of time, from the moment that Sergeyev knelt to kiss the imaginary hem of Juliet's robe and Ulanova stroked his head with infinite tenderness to that final instant when the two of them knelt together in silent marriage vows before an unseen altar, the tragic tale of Shakespeare's "star-crossed lovers" lived anew in the confines of that barren room in a dancing school in Leningrad.

A host of memories haunt the ballet school in Leningrad. That no other ballet school in the world can boast of such illustrious graduates is attested by the pictures covering the walls of the crowded, unpretentious room which serves as the school museum.

The museum director and teacher, Madame Marietta Frangopulo, escorted me from the museum to the little stage of the school's miniature theatre. "On these boards," she said, "danced such pupils as Fokine, Karsavina, Pavlova, Nijinsky and Ulanova."

Of her early days at the school, Ulanova relates: "I went there at a very difficult time. It was difficult not only because we were freezing in the cold classrooms and bedrooms; we also had very little to eat, and we were often ailing or feeling unwell.

"We exercised in huge unheated halls. It was so cold that we were allowed to wear our woolen breeches and even felt boots while making our first movements." Ulanova studied under her mother, who combined her dancing at the Mariinsky Theatre with teaching at the school. "She used to wear her light tunic, but she kept her feet in warm boots, which she took off to demonstrate various movements. Immediately after classes, she went through the corridor which linked the school with the rehearsal hall, where she herself was training every day. This example of artistic discipline served as an inspiration to the children who had just started the school."

Ulanova's mother retired from the stage in 1924 and devoted herself to teaching at the Leningrad school until she was sixty-four.

As we drove along the ice-strewn River Neva after the rehearsal, Helen Konstantinova told Ulanova that she had studied as a child to be a ballet dancer and that her teacher at the Leningrad ballet school had been Ulanova's mother. Sitting between the two of them, Helen Petrova listened with fascination as they reminisced about the past.

Later, when Ulanova had left us, Helen Konstantinova said wistfully, "She belongs to Leningrad. When will she come back to us?"

Helen Petrova had to hurry off to deliver a lecture to her students of English and American literature. She told me afterward, "What a strange lecture it was! I talked about Swift, Defoe, Fielding—and Ulanova! And the emphasis was on Ulanova. I must have spent the first fifteen minutes talking about her. I couldn't help it. You understand, don't you?"

It was to the famed Imperial Mariinsky Theatre that in 1914 Sergei Ulanov, *regisseur* of the ballet troupe, took his four-year-old daughter, Galina Sergeyevna, to see her first ballet performance. The ballet was *Sleeping Beauty*. "All would have gone off well," Ulanova recalls, "if at the appearance of the Lilac Fairy I hadn't cried out at the top of my voice, 'That's Mama, my Mama!' The general embarrassment was great. . . . Why, I couldn't understand. Hadn't I spoken the truth? The Lilac Fairy *was* my mother. I longed for everyone to know that the illustrious fairy was my own mother, mine and no one else's."

At this same theatre in October 1928, Ulanova made her debut at the age of eighteen as Princess Florina in the ballet in which she had first seen her mother dance, and here, a few months afterward, she danced her first leading role as Odette-Odile in Tchaikovsky's *Swan Lake*. . . .

Now, more than three decades later, in April 1960, when Ulanova returned to the Theatre to dance as Juliet, such was the wonder of her artistry that time dissolved; she was again a girl; and seeing her come upon the stage, one could echo Friar Laurence's words:

Here comes the lady: O! so light a foot
Will ne'er wear out the everlasting flint.

As I photographed the curtain calls during the thunderous acclaim at the end of the performance, it seemed to me there was something strange about Ulanova's attire. Later, I realized what it was. She had to hurry to catch the night train back to Moscow; she already had on her street clothes under Juliet's robe—and, instead of ballet shoes, she was wearing snow boots.

Chapter 5

Seeds and Blossoms

Reached through a shadowy gateway off a side-street near the Bolshoi Theatre, the building is weather-beaten and old. Its four stories of yellowish stucco face on a small triangular courtyard with a few spare trees. Little about the outside betokens the loveliness within.

By its very nature, the Bolshoi Ballet School is an extraordinary place. In what other art, indeed, do apprentices gather at the age of ten to devote the next decade of their lives to learning their craft? Where else will one find this youthful discipline of mind and body dedicated to a vision of creating beauty and giving joy? Ulanova, who is chairman of the school's examining board, says it is not enough "only to learn the ABC of the language of the dance.... One must also develop a certain attitude toward life itself. The work of the dancer involves not only arms and legs but also intellects and hearts. It is with this in mind that we must tend these young shoots of Soviet art."

Prior to visiting the Bolshoi Ballet School, I had always been somewhat skeptical of the phenomenon of love at first sight. But within a matter of hours, I lost my heart to not just one but a host of claimants. It was all I could do to tear myself away from the first class I attended, where beribboned twelve-year-olds were exercising with a breath-taking grace and a dedication that gave their faces an added purity. Each classroom held new enchantments—erect and manly little boys coaching one another at the *barre*; fledgling ballerinas poised in sculptural arabesques; steel-muscled youths who seemed to have mastered the secret of flight; flesh-and-blood Degas' on all sides. Even the corridors had their own heart-warming witchery: the sweetly solemn greetings from the pupils hurrying between classes, the boys bowing and girls curtseying as they murmured to me, "Greetings."

There were three hundred and fifty pupils at the school. Their nine-year course of study encompassed not only an exhaustive training in multifarious aspects of dance technique (including classical and historical dancing, folk and character dancing, mime and acting) but also a comprehensive education in regular academic subjects. Music, stagecraft, and the history of the ballet, theatre and fine arts comprised an additional part of their curriculum. The school staff, counting teachers both of dance and academic subjects, numbered almost one hundred; many of the dance teachers were present or former Bolshoi dancers. Attendance at the school was entirely free. Pupils were selected on the basis of physical suitability and talent for ballet. That year, I was told, there had been more than a thousand applicants for entrance to the school.

But noteworthy as were these facts and figures, the thing that most impressed me was the mood pervading the school. Joyfulness and discipline, diligence and creativity were so interwoven that one felt there could be no more fitting beginning for a life dedicated to the dance.

"In Czarist days," says Ulanova, "no members of minority groups were admitted to the Bolshoi school. Now any child with the ability can come. . . ."

In a school annex called the *Internat* were boarded fifty boys and girls from distant Soviet republics and foreign countries — from Kazhakistan and Korea, Azerbaijan and Albania, Uzbekistan, Lithuania, Moldavia, and China. (A newcomer was buoyant, auburn-haired, fifteen-year-old Anne Stone from Surrey, England, who had—she told me—been "frightened at first" because she spoke only English, but whose measure of adjustment after a few months was indicated by the fact that as we talked she kept lapsing unconsciously into Russian. Another foreign pupil at the school was the American Anastasia Stevens, daughter of the Moscow correspondent for *Time* Magazine.)

One morning I learned that Ulanova was paying an unexpected visit to the *Internat*. Hurrying over, I found an impromptu program of entertainment for her already under way. Seated among a group of children whose faces shone in an ecstasy of excitement and pride, she responded to the performances with an enthusiasm matching theirs. None of the youngsters applauded the songs and dances more spiritedly or laughed with greater relish at the humorous skits. The children, who obviously regarded her as the sum of everything wonderful in the world, watched her every gesture adoringly.

The performance over, Ulanova was invited to address her youthful hosts. When she agreed, a murmur of excitement ran through the room. Then, all at once, there was absolute silence. On tiptoe, one of the boys brought a chair to the center of the floor. Ulanova did not use it for its intended purpose. As she spoke, she stood behind it, her hands restlessly moving across its top, occasionally tipping it from side to side. Her tone contained no hint that she was addressing children. Only afterward, when I looked over my notes, did it occur to me that she had spoken so as to be understood by every child in the room.

She began by talking about her own childhood. "When I was small and anyone asked me what I wanted to be, I'd immediately say, 'A boy!' Sometimes I'd add I wanted to be a sailor too." The children laughed delightedly. "The games I liked best were boys' games, and almost all of my friends were boys. I used to pretend the woods where we played were a thick jungle and my friends were faithful companions in some mysterious, unexplored country." Her longing to be a boy, she said, stemmed from the influence of her

father, an ardent hunter and fisherman who loved the out-of-doors. "Watching him, I became convinced that what I regarded as girl's occupations were not meant for me. . . . Even after I was at ballet school, I wanted to dance male roles. I knew all the ways of supporting a female partner. Sometimes I actually took boys' parts on the stage, and I liked that especially. . . ."

Growing more serious, she said that her mother had been the decisive influence in her career not only as her "first teacher and constant adviser" but also as "the best example of a ballerina's attitude toward her profession." Learning to dance, she said, had not been easy for her. "For one thing, my legs were weak. Yes," she added, seeing the incredulous expressions of her listeners, "they were very weak. In fact, when I danced in my first performances, the stage workers sometimes wondered if they wouldn't break!" At that, there was an audible gasp in the room. "The training at the school was hard for me, the long drills and the seemingly endless work at the *barre*. . . . Later on, too, when I was grown-up and it was summer, vacation time, I often wanted to get away from the *barre* and join my friends swimming in the lake or paddling a canoe. But afterward I'd feel happy I hadn't shirked my duty, and when my work was done I'd know I had the right to join my friends and enjoy myself. Yes, a dancer must keep working, always working."

Not a child stirred as she continued. "Always remember that the smallest detail, things that may seem insignificant at first, must be done well. No matter what you're doing, whether it's dancing or singing or studying, you must try to do it better. Never be satisfied. I still work hard, and I still have a lot to learn.

"Of course, work alone isn't enough. You must seek the beauty in life. And you must make things more beautiful. You must use your mind and imagination, and not only work but create. Then you will find that life becomes more interesting and happier all the time. Then you will achieve what you want."

When Ulanova finished, the children surged about her. A bouquet of flowers materialized among them and bobbed toward her, but the ceremony obviously planned for this moment was lost amid exuberant chatter, continuing applause, and the scurrying of boys vying for the privilege of helping their cherished guest into her coat.

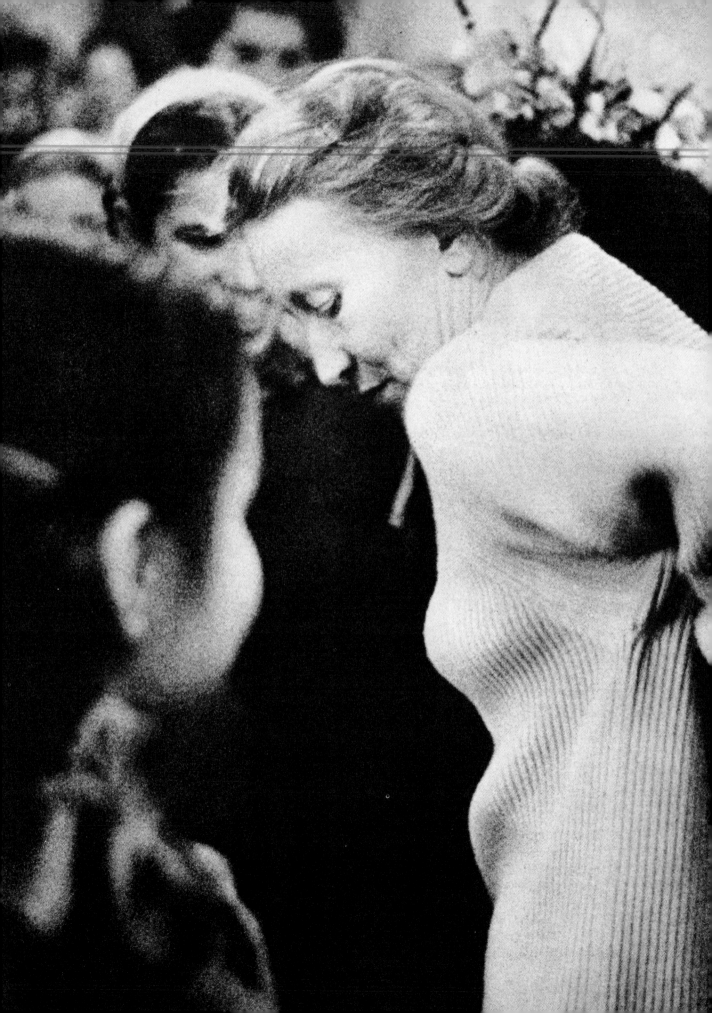

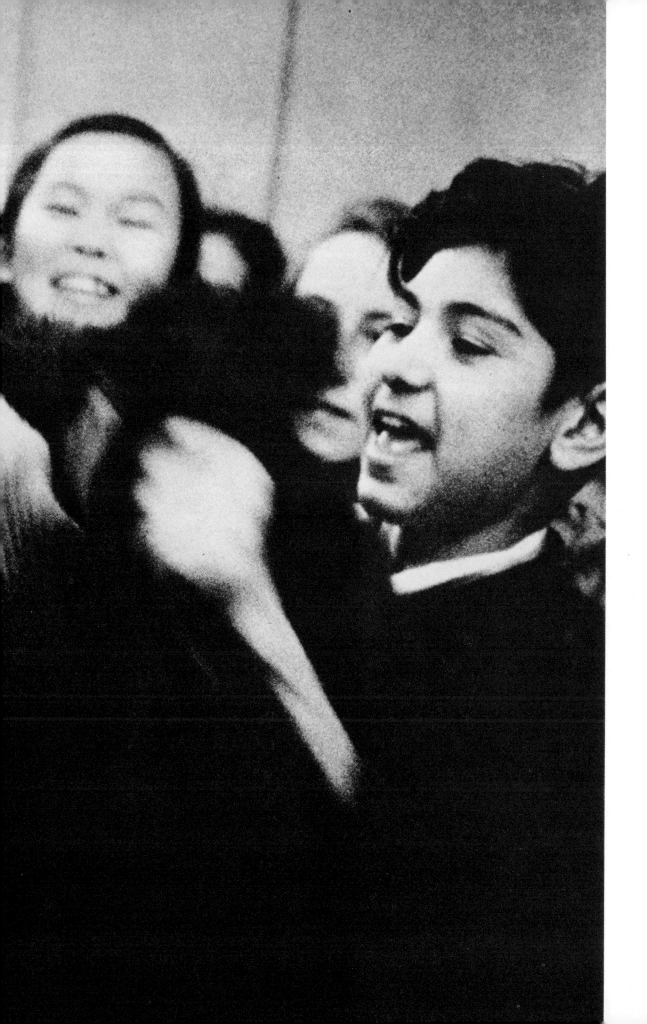

During the last days of April, the classrooms at the Bolshoi School were strangely still and the corridors deserted. In the large hall on the top floor, the most momentous event of the school year was under way—final examinations. For four morning sessions the graduating students demonstrated what they had learned of the dance during their nine years of apprenticeship.

At the examinations I attended, the examining commission included, as always, outstanding figures in the Soviet ballet world. Among them were Bolshoi choreographer Leonid Lavrovsky, *maître de ballet* Asaf Messerer, the renowned former ballerina Marina Semyonova, the school principal Sophia Golovkina, and Ulanova, chairman of the examining commission.

Her face mirroring her concentration, Ulanova rarely stirred throughout the hours of the examination. Only occasionally, reacting to some detail of special interest, did she make some remark to her close friend, the former Bolshoi dancer Nadia Kapustina, or to Deputy Minister of Culture Alexander Kuznetsov, who were usually seated beside her.

Of Ulanova's method of appraising the youthful dancers in the discussions following the examinations, one of her colleagues on the examining commission told me: "She evaluates the dancing not just as an isolated phenomenon but within a broad framework of teaching as well as performance. You might say she judges the teachers as well as the students. She's completely objective. She speaks gently but she's very strict in her judgment, just as she's very strict with herself."

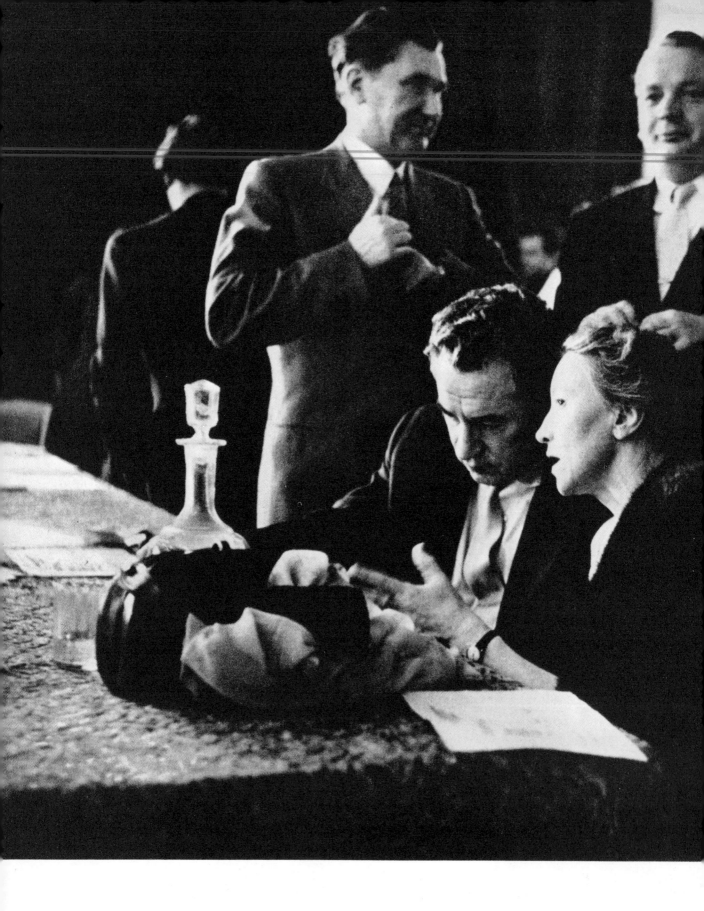

Shortly after the final examinations at the school, a gala event took place at the Bolshoi Theatre—an entire performance devoted to the work of the school, including not only the graduates but the pupils of all classes. The theatre was packed with relatives of the pupils, Bolshoi School teachers, dancers, government officials and distinguished figures in the Soviet cultural world.

Together with dancer Yuri Kondratov and other teachers, Ulanova sat in the director's box contemplatively watching the performance; and at its end, when all the pupils gathered on the stage, first bowing to the audience and then flinging flowers in the air, she joined warmly in the applause that thundered in the theatre.

Chapter 6

Precious Heritage

A teacher affects eternity...

—Henry Adams

In the transient instant of the dance, the present becomes the past even while the now is here. This oldest of the arts is also the most evanescent; and complementing that paradox is the fact that the ballet, which transcends all language barriers, has no accepted written language of its own. Like the poetry of ancient bards, its legacy is handed down from one generation to the next, from one master to another. Hence the uniquely vital function of the teacher of ballet.

"The work of the instructor is an art, and what a great art!" Ulanova wrote some years ago, commenting on the influence of her own teachers. "The artist creates the role, the teacher molds the personality of the artist into one capable of creating an artistic image. . . . Let us not discuss who is the more important. Let us agree that the work of the artist and the work of the teacher are both arts."

Today Ulanova herself has become a teacher, and in her the art of instruction finds its quintessence. To watch her teaching one of her pupils is to witness the bestowal of a precious heritage and the evocation of new beauty.

It was shortly after arriving in Moscow that I learned for the first time about Ulanova's work as a teacher. I did not learn about it from her. During our early chats, she said nothing of this notable new phase of her career. Characteristically, she preferred to let others do the talking.

This time my source of information was Georgi Orvid, Director of the Bolshoi. We were talking one morning about the schedule at the Theatre when, quite casually, he mentioned that Ulanova was now devoting much time to teaching certain young ballerinas and preparing them for important roles. Seeing my immediate interest, he went on to name several of her pupils. One was the nineteen-year-old Katya Maximova, whose dancing as a soloist had stirred excited comment when the Bolshoi Ballet toured the United States the previous summer, barely a year after her graduation from ballet school. "Ulanova," said Orvid, "is coaching Katya for her debut in *Giselle*."

I lost no time in telling Ulanova of my eagerness to photograph her working with Maximova. Her reply was indicative of her attitude toward her pupil. "It all depends on how Maximova feels about it," she said. "It might disturb her." Fortunately, Maximova raised no objections.

The pictures in this chapter were taken over a period of many weeks. When I began photographing Ulanova instructing Maximova, it was midwinter (the season being indicated, somewhat incongruously, by the neat little snow boots Ulanova occasionally wore while practicing with her pupil); and, as the warm winds of spring sauntered through Moscow and children planted flowers in Sverdlov Square, the combined labors of teacher and pupil continued until that long-anticipated day in June when Maximova finally gave her first performance as Giselle. They met several times a week, usually in the early afternoon after Ulanova had finished her own classwork and rehearsals, and they worked together for an hour either in one of the fourth-floor classrooms or in a dance studio in the Theatre wing.

Ulanova's method of teaching had strangely paradoxical qualities. On the one hand, there was nothing didactic about it; such was her intimate rapport with Maximova and utter lack of condescension that I was rarely conscious of a teacher-pupil relationship between the world-famous ballerina and her teen-age protégée. Indeed, their co-ordination of effort sometimes fostered the illusion that the two of them were one, that Ulanova moved not only beside but inside Maximova. On the other hand, Ulanova's scrutiny of

Maximova's work was so objective that she seemed, for all her absorption and tender regard for her pupil, to be watching as if from a great distance and without the slightest personal bias. When she counseled Maximova, it was with a gentle quietness that carried no clue to her compressed intensity of feeling. Despite the multiple demands upon her at the time and the inner tension under which she was working, I never once saw her display the least sign of impatience with Maximova.

Having written of the art of teaching in terms of the molding of a pupil, Ulanova brought that image vividly to life. The expressive, ever-varying motions of her hands as she coached Maximova had a sculptural quality, as if her fervent fingers were shaping some invisible form. Without wishing to sound mystical, I must say that often it appeared as if, like a sorceress, Ulanova were summoning forth some secret spirit from her pupil's inmost being. (For those who may be inclined—like Ulanova herself, no doubt—to smile at such a concept, I suggest consideration of the photograph on the immediately preceding pages.)

For me, watching Ulanova teach was as endlessly fascinating as watching her practice; and for her, my fascination with the one was just as mystifying as with the other. "What, again?" she would say, eyebrows quizzically raised, at my continual appearances at her sessions with Maximova. "But it will be the same as last time."

Of course, it never was. As with her classwork, there was always something new, some incident or gesture or expression, some singularly lovely moment that cried out to be recorded. Not that my presence always made this possible. Once, for example, I was reloading a camera when Ulanova—who from time to time assumed various supporting roles to Maximova's Giselle and was then taking the mother's part—embraced Maximova with such infinite tenderness that I felt compelled to do something I had never done before. I asked Ulanova to repeat the episode. "It was such a beautiful moment," I told her.

She said with a mischievous smile, "That beautiful moment is gone forever." Then she added, "Now you mustn't interrupt us. We're working." She spoke good-naturedly enough, but there was no doubting she meant precisely what she said. My camera was tolerated as long as it was forgotten and intruded in no way on their work. And that was essential for me too; otherwise I could not have captured a fragment of the truth.

When it came to discussing her work with Ulanova, Ekaterina Maximova was girlishly shy, but what she said was memorable.

"Ulanova," she related, "says a dancer must learn to express thoughts in movements so convincingly that movements are like words and dancing is as expressive as speech. If you ask her how to achieve this, she smiles and tells you there's no formula for creating beauty. It's necessary, she says, to keep searching and always working, always working. . . .

"Yes, that's what she stresses most of all—work. She keeps telling me, 'Work, work, work. Without work, there is nothing.' "

Of her first lesson with Ulanova, Maximova recalls, "I was very nervous when I learned that Ulanova would prepare me for the role of Giselle. I had seen Galina Sergeyevna on the stage, of course, when I was a pupil at the Bolshoi School, and she visited the school and was present at our final exams. Sometimes, when we were still pupils, we were lucky enough to take part in performances with her—as in *Cinderella*, when we were the dancing birds. And afterward, when I graduated and joined the Bolshoi, I danced in ballets with her. Even so, I was nervous about working with her. But Galina Sergeyevna came and she just smiled a good smile and said, 'Well, let's start working,' and somehow my nervousness disappeared, and so we started working together."

In the final phases of their work on *Giselle*, Ulanova and Maximova were periodically joined by the well-known conductor Gennadi Rozhdestvensky, who was to lead the orchestra on the night of Maximova's debut. Despite his youthfulness (he was only thirty), Rozhdestvensky had

already been a full conductor for eight years.

Yuri Zhdanov, who was Ulanova's partner in *Romeo and Juliet* and was to dance with Maximova in *Giselle*, also joined in the rehearsals. Soon afterward, they moved to full rehearsals on the big stage.

"Of course," relates Maximova, "not every-thing was always all right with my work. But Galina Sergeyevna would explain my mistakes to me very patiently and in a very friendly way. She emphasized that I should think about the char-acter—the image—of Giselle all the time and that I should make myself really feel the tragedy of this girl."

To heighten Maximova's understanding of the role and attune her mood, Ulanova recommended that she read various literary classics of a poetic and romantic nature.

In Ulanova's words: "I wanted to develop her imagination. Without that, an artist has no being. I wanted to help Katya to think creatively. I don't know any better way to help a young artist."

196

There was no aspect of Maximova's preparation for her debut that Ulanova did not personally supervise with painstaking care. When the time came for Maximova's costume fitting, Ulanova accompanied her to the Bolshoi Craft Shops and checked every detail of her costume with a solicitude that made one think of a mother choosing her daughter's wedding dress.

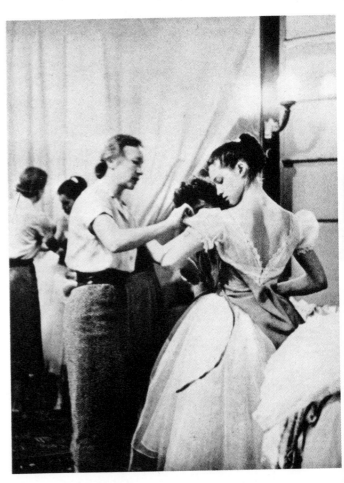

As the day of Maximova's debut approached, it was difficult to decide who was the more nervous —Maximova or Ulanova. I was, in fact, reminded of a story Ulanova had told about her own debut in *Swan Lake*. "No excitement of mine," she had related, "could compare with my mother's anxiety. She was doubly anxious, because as my teacher she was thoroughly familiar with every difficult movement and with my weak points. . . . Imagine what she felt when I had to perform the thirty-two *fouettés* in the third act! She left the seat in her box and went to the rear in order to pray for me. . . . At every debut of mine, even at every ordinary performance, when the dance con-tained some technically intricate movement, my mother would put her head down, cover her face with her hands and look at the stage through her fingers."

Of her opening night in *Giselle*, Maximova later said: "I really find it hard to remember just what happened. . . . But I'll never forget Ulanova's concern. She didn't go to the box. She was in my dressing room until the performance began and between the acts. During the performance she stayed in the wings, and every time I had to go on stage she cheered me up. I think my happiest moment was when she congratulated me afterward."

Chapter 7

Among the Birches

All impressions of life," writes Ulanova, "settle in our minds, and the strongest, the most vivid and the most beautiful imperceptibly influence the development of what we call artistry...."

Of life's myriad impressions, none has had a more lasting influence on Ulanova than her love of nature. Perhaps the happiest recollections of her youth are associated with the countryside. "It was through my father," she relates, "that I found the beauty of the forest. It was really he who taught me to love the out-of-doors....He didn't talk a great deal—even when we were alone together. But he did more important things. He took me with him when he went fishing or hunting before sunrise. How much we saw together! The sun coming up and its glow shredding the cold mist, paths almost hidden in the woods, flowers all wet with dew, the great blue sky....And how much my future work gained from all of this! Of course, I didn't think then about 'the importance of learning to love nature,' and if I had, its fascination would probably have promptly disappeared."

For Ulanova, nature has never lost its fascination, nor she her passion for the out-of-doors. She is, I think, happiest when in the country. And one senses more—that here, among her beloved flowers, lakes and forests, she finds a source of sustenance, a realm of replenishment in the process of creation.

From time to time, though certainly not as often as she would like, Ulanova manages to find a day when she can get away for a few hours. Then, accompanied by the prancing, bright-eyed Bolshoi, whose delight at these expeditions rivals her own, she drives into the country to one of several familiar retreats. Perhaps her favorite is a magnificent birch forest set like a silver island among gentle waves of fields near the village of Barvija.

No tree is more indigenous to the landscape of Russia or closer to the hearts of its people than the birch. For this reason alone, the forest near Barvija would seem a particularly appropriate setting for Ulanova. I found it so for an additional reason. Between her and the dappled trees, whose slender trunks reached skyward with an airy lightness, there was an affinity of elegance and grace. As she moved among them, playing hide-and-seek with the gleefully cavorting Bolshoi and picking flowers for Vadim to paint, she seemed a bright and integral part of the forest's design.

In recent years, with increasingly frequent Bolshoi Ballet tours abroad, Ulanova has had to snatch brief vacations between trips to Japan and Austria, France and Italy, Germany and Great Britain, the United States and China. The summer of 1960 was a welcome exception; she and Rindin were taking a full two months' vacation. They spent it at a friend's *dacha* on the outskirts of the village of Mozjenka, about fifty miles from Moscow. (It is typical of the striking simplicity of their lives that, unlike many Soviet artists, they have no *dacha* of their own.)

On a warm Sunday morning in mid-July, I drove out through the tranquil wooded countryside surrounding Moscow, past fields patterned with Brueghelesque groups of picnickers, to visit Ulanova and Rindin at Mozjenka. The brief two weeks since the end of the Bolshoi season had wrought a striking transformation in Ulanova. In a loose-fitting white jacket, gayly flowered dress and well-worn sneakers, with ruddy cheeks and hair in gentle disarray, she contrasted sharply with the intense, preoccupied individual whose work I had watched week after week at the Bolshoi.

When I told her I'd never seen her look so rested, she replied, "Why shouldn't I? For once, all I'm doing is resting. Swimming, reading and lying in the sun—that's my work schedule." Her only other occupation, she said as we sat on a porch overlooking a lovely garden, was studying French with her friend Nadia Kapustina, who was spending the vacation with her. "I haven't even started to skip rope yet. Vadim is the only one who's working." She pointed to the canvases of his landscapes.

I asked Ulanova how long it would take her to get back into dancing condition in the fall.

"It usually takes about the same amount of time as I rest. So I'll have to work for six or eight weeks before any performances. But it's too peaceful here to think about that now. . . ."

There had, however, been one disturbance of the peace. A few days ago, she related, Bolshoi had disappeared for several hours.

"The dog, not the theatre," interjected Rindin.

"No one knows where he went," continued Ulanova, quite solemnly. "He's under restrictions now. He has to stay close to the house, except when he's with me." Picking up Bolshoi and indicating to him the general direction of his recent excursion, she affectionately warned him against any recurrence of it.

After lunch, we strolled across the neighboring meadows, down a wooded gully, and through a flourishing cornfield to the banks of the Moscow River, whose upper reaches wind past Mozjenka. "It's a most obliging river," said Rindin. "In winter it flows past our apartment and in summer past our *dacha*."

Ulanova said she came to swim here early each morning. Now it was Bolshoi's turn. He swam back and forth proudly retrieving sticks for his mistress. His pleasure, however, was comparatively short-lived. After scrutinizing his shaggy ears, which had a propensity for collecting burrs and other miscellanea, Ulanova proceeded to wash them methodically and then squeeze the water out of them—an operation which Bolshoi, for all his resigned mien, enjoyed no more than most youngsters of his age.

Rindin suggested we visit the Savastorjojevsky Monastery at the nearby village of Zvenigorod. As we were driving over, Ulanova suddenly pointed down the highway toward two cyclists and said, "Look who's coming!" The cyclists were ballerina Nina Timofieva and conductor Gennadi Rozhdestvensky. Only a few days before, they had been in London with the Bolshoi Ballet.

A vociferous reunion took place at the side of the road. Timofieva gave a lively account of their experiences in England and, from a bundle strapped on her bicycle, produced a book of

paintings by Van Gogh, which she showed Ulanova. Meanwhile, with a somewhat alarming disregard for passing vehicles, Rindin and Rozhdestvensky darted about the group, assuming various extravagant poses with their cameras in a gleeful parody of my photographic efforts.

Situated on a wooded knoll, its golden cupolas gleaming above crenelated walls, the Savastorjojevsky Monastery brooded over the surrounding countryside like a lonely sentinel from the past. As we walked through ponderous archways and shadowy crypts paved with ancient flagstones, Rindin told me that the monastery had been built in the fourteenth century and, like many in medieval times, had served both as a retreat for the devout and a fortress against marauding invaders. The piles of brick and rubble and the scaffolding on the buildings were mute reminders of a more recent invader. "The Nazis almost completely destroyed it," said Rindin. "We're reconstructing it now."

The imagination is a weak instrument in comparison with experience. Looking at the strolling families in the monastery on that peaceful Sunday afternoon, with cloud puffs drifting overhead and foliage stirring lazily on the hillsides, I found it difficult to conceive of those dark and agonizing days when the Nazi Army had occupied the very soil on which I now stood.

Perhaps that past seemed all the more remote and unimaginable because of the nobility and beauty of the human spirit, which, in Ulanova, had held my mind and eye for months.

Principal Dates in Ulanova's Career

1910   Born, January 10, St. Petersburg*

1919   Entered State School of Choreography (formerly the Imperial School and later the Leningrad School)

1928   Graduation from the Leningrad School of Choreography. Joined ballet troupe of State Theatre of Opera and Ballet (formerly the Mariinsky Theatre and later the Kirov Theatre). Debut: *The Sleeping Beauty*

1929   Performances in *Swan Lake, Nutcracker* and *The Sleeping Beauty*

1930   *Première* of new ballet, *The Age of Gold*

1931   Performances in *Raymonda, Le Corsaire, The Snow Maiden* and *Chopiniana*

1932-35   Performances in *Giselle, The Flame of Paris* (première 1932), *The Hump-Backed Horse, Swan Lake, Nutcracker, The Fountain of Bakhchisarai, Esmeralda,* and *Chopiniana*

1936   Performance in *première* of *Lost Illusions*

1939   Awarded the Order of the Labor Red Banner. Granted title of Honored Artist of the USSR.

1940   Performances in *première* of new ballet, *Romeo and Juliet,* and *Swan Lake.* Awarded the Badge of Honor by Supreme Soviet of the USSR and granted honorary title of National Artist of the USSR.

1941   *Première* of *La Bayadère.* Performances at the Bolshoi Theatre in Moscow. Awarded Stalin Prize for outstanding services in the development of ballet art

1941-42   Performances with Kirov ballet troupe at Molotov. Work with Kazakh State Theatre of Opera and Ballet at Alma-Ata

1944   Joined ballet company of the Bolshoi Theatre

1945   *Première* of new ballet, *Cinderella*

1946   Moscow *première* of *Romeo and Juliet.* Awarded Stalin Prize for performance in role of Cinderella; medal "For Valiant Labor in the Patriotic War"; and medal "For the Defense of Leningrad"

1947   Awarded Stalin Prize for performance in role of Juliet

1948   Performances in Leningrad, Kiev, Tallinn, Minsk

1949   Performances in Hungary and Czechoslovakia. New production of *Red Poppy* in Moscow

1950   Performances in Italy

1952   Performances in China

1953   Films: *Swan Lake* and *Fountains of Bakhchisarai*

1954   New version of *Stone Flower* in Moscow; Berlin performance; film, *Romeo and Juliet*

1956   Film, *Giselle;* performance in London

1957   Awarded Lenin Prize

1958   Performances in Paris, Brussels, Hamburg and Munich

1959   Performances in United States, Canada and China

1960   Final Bolshoi Theatre performance

1961   Performances in Egypt and Hungary. Retirement from stage. Assumes post of artistic coach at Bolshoi Theatre.

*St. Petersburg was the capital of Czarist Russia. The name of the city was changed to Petrograd at the outbreak of the First World War and in 1924 to Leningrad.

Acknowledgments

While the photographs and text in this book are mine, it is in a very real sense a co-operative effort. So many individuals assisted me that this note of acknowledgment inevitably is something of a frustration: I cannot record my indebtedness to each one personally, as I would like to.

The work could not have been accomplished without the extensive aid I received from a number of organizations and institutions in the Soviet Union. I am greatly indebted to the artists, technicians and administrative staff of the Bolshoi Theatre, who assisted me in innumerable ways while the book was in the making; and to the officials of the Ministry of Culture, the State Committee for Cultural Relations with Foreign Countries, the Union of Societies for Friendly and Cultural Relations with Foreign Countries, and Foreign Literature Publishers, who took a warm personal interest in the project and greatly facilitated it. I must also express my appreciation to the State Bakhroushin Museum of the Theatre, for valuable research materials placed at my disposal; to the Pravda Photo Laboratory, for generous assistance in technical phases of my photography; to the Soviet Peace Committee, for arranging for the translation of Ulanova's writings; and to the Bolshoi Ballet School, whose teachers and pupils coupled eager co-operation with heartwarming hospitality. My thanks are due to the Leningrad School of Ballet for providing me with data regarding the early years of Ulanova's career.

As indicated in my prefatory note, Peter Schwed of Simon and Schuster helped me get the book under way; and throughout the undertaking his friendly encouragement was unflagging. From William Collins of Collins Publishers in England I also received enthusiastic support.

During my work, I repeatedly turned to Arnold Haskell for guidance and advice, and I owe him much for counsel no less inspiring than wise. Charlotte Seitlin, Edith Fowler and Helen Barrow, of Simon and Schuster, made most helpful suggestions regarding the format and text of the book, as did Mark Bonham-Carter of Collins Publishers. Modernage Custom Darkrooms handled the printing and enlargement of my photographs with gratifying care.

I must record a special indebtedness to Otto and Hansel Hagel for their warm and indispensable assistance. I wish also to express my appreciation of the valuable aid given to me by Carolyn Parks of the San Francisco Academy of Ballet, and Leona Norman of the San Rafael Ballet School; and to thank Jo Sinel, Angus Cameron, Tamara Mamedova, Eugene Umnov, Vera Shevjakova and Lydia Moroshkina for their generous help.

I am very grateful to Robert W. Dowling for making it possible for my photographs of Ulanova to become a permanent part of the Dance Collection at the New York Public Library.

And to Riette, my wife, I must express special gratitude for her unremitting and invaluable assistance in all phases of my work.

A.E.K.

About the Author

A writer of singular versatility, Albert E. Kahn had earned a celebrated international reputation for his political exposés prior to his widely acclaimed work on Galina Ulanova. His book Sabotage!, dealing with Fascist conspiratorial activities, was one of the top best-sellers of the Second World War; and his subsequent books on secret diplomacy and the Cold War era have been translated into more than twenty languages. Among his recent works is the noted Joys and Sorrows—Reflections by Pablo Casals, as told to Albert E. Kahn. Permanent collections of his photographic studies of Ulanova and Casals are housed at the Library and Museum of the Performing Arts at Lincoln Center, New York; the San Francisco Museum of Art; and the Dartmouth College Library.

Born in London, England, Mr. Kahn is a graduate of Dartmouth College. He is married, has three sons, and lives in Glen Ellen, California.